— Bodie Today —

Painting of Bodie buildings by W. Lee Symmonds.

Bodie of 1879. Neither the M. E. nor Catholic Church had been built. Since it was a time exposure photograph, neither humans or animals can be seen although thousands were living there at the time.

Courtesy of California State Library

Printed and Distributed
by Chalfant Press, Inc.
Bishop, California
for
Sierra Media, Inc.
Bishop, California
Copyright 1967 — Sierra Media, Inc.
15th Printing 1977

Library of Congress Card Number: 67-31002

ACKNOWLEDGEMENTS

While searching for facts and photographs on Bodie, not only did we learn to love the old Ghost Town but also were touched by the spontaneous cooperation and good will extended to us not only by individuals but also by those in charge of both public and private archives.

Letters, newspapers and original papers are important source material on the old mining camps and are to be found in the museums and libraries. We are most grateful to the personnel of all those we visited for their cheerful cooperation and help. We are indebted to the following persons and institutions: John H. Michael, Norman Wilson and Allen Welts of the California Department of Parks and Recreation, Division of Beaches and Parks; Norman Cleaver and John Myers, Bodie State Park; Allan R. Ottley, R. Clauson, Mrs. Mary Coulter, California State Library; Miss Ruth I. Mahood and Russell E. Belous, History Division, Los Angeles County Museum and also the Library Staff at the Los Angeles County Museum; John Barr Thompkins and staff, Bancroft Library, University of California at Berkeley; James De T. Abajian and Bill Burtis, California Historical Society Library; W. Lee Symmonds and William J. Glenn, Mono County Museum; Mrs. Clara S. Beatty and staff, Nevada Historical Society; J. W. Calhoun and staff, Nevada State Museum; Dwight Warren, Death Valley Museum, Death Valley National Monument; H. Hamlin, editor of The PONY EXPRESS; and the Eastern California Museum.

Bodieites and collectors of Bodie material were especially generous not only with their time and help but also in sharing their photographs so that we all can see the Bodie of yesteryear. Our heartfelt thanks to William J. Glenn; the McDonell sisters (Mrs. Alice McDonell Smith, Jeannette McDonell Colvin and Dorothy McDonell Coffin); William Young; John Myers; Cecil Burkham; Mrs. Ruth Burkham; Bruce Burkham; George M. Metzger; Fred S. Brooks; Mrs. Floris E. Harris; C. Lorin Ray; Mrs. Esther Brunk; Mervin McKenzie.

Special thanks to John McLaren Forbes and Mrs. A. A. Forbes for their cooperation; Jack Moffett, who entered into the spirit of old Bodie with his pen and ink sketches; W. Lee Symmonds, who not only painted the cover but also assisted us in his capacity as Historian of the Mono County Museum.

Cover painting of Methodist Church in Bodie by W. Lee Symmonds.
Backcover: All photos by author except cemetery scene by Esther Brunk.
Pen and Ink Sketches by Jack Moffett.

To the Editors and Photographers of bygone days

The old time editors were personalities in themselves which was reflected in their papers. They taunted each other and the neighboring camps but always extolled the virtues and wealth of their own camps. Writers and correspondents wrote in the idiom of the day. "The camp that lasted soon"; "A lively camp"; "The Esmeralda excitement"; or the "Bodie excitement"—all these gave us a feeling of the life and times. We decided in order not to lose this special essence we would use the items intact. We hope that you too will enjoy this living spirit of Bodie as it was perpetuated by the mining camp editors and photographers.

Grant H. Smith describes Bodie during its greatest excitement—1879 and 1880.

The traffic in the streets was continuous and enlivening. There were trains of huge, white-topped "prairie-schooners," bringing freight from the railroad, each drawn by twenty or more horses or mules, and pulling one or two large, four-wheeled "trailers"; ore-wagons, hauling ore down the canyon to the mills; wood wagons bringing huge loads of pine-nut wood from long distances, for the mines and mills and for general use; hay wagons, lumber wagons, prospecting outfits, nondescript teams of all descriptions, spanking teams driven by mine superintendents, horses ridden by everybody, and most exciting of all, the daily stages that came tearing into town and went rushing out; the outgoing stages often carrying bars of bullion, guarded by stern, silent men, armed with sawed-off shotguns loaded with buckshot, who did not always succeed in protecting their treasure.

"Bodie: The Last of the Old-Time Mining Camps" appeared in Volume IV, No. 1, of the California Historical Society QUARTERLY.

The Ghost Town of BODIE

As Reported in the Newspapers of the Day.

by
Russ and Anne Johnson

BODIE, CAL. 1878

FORBES.

FORBES.

Bodie Dedication

Bodie lives again! Once again is heard the laughter of children; there is traffic on the streets; the sounds of voices drift between the buildings.

To the ghosts of 1879 who might be hovering in the buildings of Bodie, this new life of Bodie will seem most sedate. These sounds will not compare to their memories of the thump of stamp mills going day and night, the whistles of the hoisting works, the sing-song chant of the Chinese wood gatherers, the squeak and rattle of teams and wagons, the shouts of the teamsters or the noise emanating out of the saloons.

Bodie lives again because of the diligence and the faith of J. S. Cain and his family. The Cain family spearheaded the project to preserve and protect Bodie. Because of their leadership and the support of the many other interested people, Bodie has become a California State Park, a State Historical Landmark and a National Historic Site.

Bodie lives again for the enjoyment of the many who will come to visit this California State Park.

The California Division of Beaches and Parks personnel live in Bodie summer and winter. Summer, when they are joined by thousands of visitors; winter, when the snow storms isolate them from all traffic. In addition to sharing their knowledge of the colorful history of Bodie with the visitors, these Park Rangers work to maintain and preserve the Ghost Town of Bodie for the enjoyment of future generations.

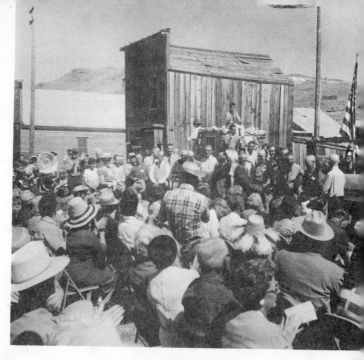

The Dedication of the Ghost Town of Bodie was held on September 12, 1964. Superior Court Judge Walter R. Evans was master of ceremonies, with Rev. Orville F. Blackburn delivering the invocation. Walter B. Cain, chairman of Mono County Board of Supervisors, gave

he welcoming remarks, especially welcoming former Bodie residents. Many Bodieites, either those who had been born there or those who had resided there, attended the ceremonies and were the honored guests of the day. Dignitaries as well as senior citizens were paid tribute, including Ella and Victor Cain who kept Bodie intact. The J. S. Cain Memorial plaque was accepted by Mrs. Ella M. Cain. Congressman Harold T. "Bizz" Johnson was on hand to accept the National Historic Landmark plaque from Dr. John A. Hussey, Regional Chief, Division of History and Archeology, National Park Service, U. S. Dept. of Interior. Charles A. DeTurk, Director of the State Dept. of Parks and Recreation, presented the State Historical Landmark plaque, formally accepted by Edward F. Dolder, Chief, State Division of Beaches and Parks. State Senator William F. Symons, reviewed history of Bodie and traced development of Bodie as a state park site.

State Senator Paul J. Lunardi (representing Mono County) and Jack McCloskey, a Hawthorne, Nevada publisher (representing Mineral County, Nevada) were delegated to settle the mock dispute of the jurisdiction of the California-Nevada border counties. There was a "shoot down" between California Senator John C. Begovich and Nevada Senator Bruck Parks. Col. Frank R. Wilkerson, Commander of the U.S.M.C. at Pickel Meadows was forced to bring this affair to a halt.

The Marine Band, First Marine Division, F. M. F., Camp Pendleton was flown in especially for the occasion. Hunewill Guest Ranch furnished riders in costume. Members of E Clampus Vitus, California '49er Historical and Humbug Society were on hand, as were Bridgeport and Mono County Chambers of Commerce. Many persons dressed in the costume of the era which added to the festive air. The Benediction was delivered by Father Thomas V. Savage.

Bodie Post Office and Bodie Bank before 1932 fire.
Courtesy of Bancroft Libr[...]

EVENING MINER.

THE MONO COUNTY BANK.

Bodie, Mono County, California; organized in 1877.

Capital Stock : : $100,000

President.....................ROBERT BARTON
Vice President...............WM. S. HOPKINS

Transacts a General Banking and Exchange Business.
Exchange on Eastern States and Europe.

Stocks Bought and Sold

On the San Francisco Stock Exchange, by telegraph,
on commission. Dividends collected and assessments
paid. apt   H. F. HASTINGS, Cashier.

CENTRAL SALOON.

Property of the U. S. Mint, S. F.

T. M. LUTHER & CO.,
ASSAYERS,

MAIN STREET.........................BODIE.

BULLION ASSAYS GUARANTEED TO
conform accurately with the standard of
the United States Mint. Returns made in bars
or coin.

GOLD DUST BOUGHT.
1tf

The Bodie Bank

Bodie Cal. June 26" 1881

Pay to the order of Miss John Gillson

Dollars

The Bank of California
San Francisco, Cal.

Geo H Winterburn   CASHIER.

WELLS, FARGO & CO'S EXPRESS.

VALUE, $70 72/76

Bodie, Cal., August 27th 1883.

RECEIVED of The Bodie Con. Mg. Co.
Two bars Bullion
Valued at Seventy Hundred & Seventy-two 76/100 Dollars
Addressed Geo. H Sessions Secty. Bodie Con. Mg Co.
San Francisco, Cal

MONEY RECEIPT

which we undertake to forward, by usual conveyance, to the nearest point to destination reached by this Company, subject to the following conditions, namely: 1 This Company is not to be liable for any loss by the dangers of navigation, nor by
the hazards or dangers incident to a state of war; nor for any default or negligence of any person, corporation or association, to whom the above described
property shall or may be delivered by this Company, in the performance of any act or duty in respect thereto, at any place or point off the established
routes or lines of this Company; and any such person, corporation or association is not to be regarded, deemed or taken to be the agent of this Company
for any such purpose, but on the contrary, such person, corporation or association in this Company received the property above described; nor shall this Company be liable on any shipment for
an amount exceeding FIFTY DOLLARS, unless the true value thereof is herein stated.
THE PARTY ACCEPTING THIS RECEIPT HEREBY AGREES TO THE FOREGOING CONDITIONS.

For the Company,

CHARGES, $ Chg'd A/c   J C Venter

Body - Bodey - Bodie

There are many variations about the discovery of gold by Bodey as there are variations to the spelling of his name. Historians record his name variously as William S. Body, "Dutch" William S. Bodey, Watterman "Bill" Body, Waterman S. "Bill" Body. They seem to agree that Bodey came to California on the sloop Matthew Vassar in 1848, leaving his wife and family in Poughkeepsie, New York. Placer mining having declined on the west side of the Sierra, Bodey was attracted to the Monoville-Dogtown excitement and crossed over to the east side by Sonora Pass. Apparently he was accompanied by Garraty, Doyle and "Black" Taylor and some say, also by Brodigan. In July 1859 Bodey and his companions were returning from one of their exploration trips when they discovered gold and made their first location as placer ground, not as ore in place. The partners thought so well of the gold showings that they constructed a cabin in what became known as Taylor Gulch. The winter of 1859 was most severe with freezing weather

This "zebra" photograph taken from Bodie Bluff shows Bodie in early spring.
A. A. Forbes Photo   Courtesy of John Myers

and many blizzards. In March 1860 Taylor and Bodey left for Mono-ville to replenish their supplies. Returning in a blinding snowstorm, Bodey became weakened and Taylor attempted to carry him.

W. A. Chalfant in OUTPOSTS OF CIVILIZATION continues" . . . His cabinmate, "Black" (more formally E. S.) Taylor, carried the weakened man as long as he could, then wrapped him in a blanket and hastened on to their abode. When he returned, and though he hunted through the night, he could not find among the mounds, fash-ioned by the fast-falling snow on the hillside boulders, the one which covered his comrade. And there rested the discoverer until the sun of another spring melted away the chill mantle."

When the snow melted in May 1860, Body was found and buried in a shallow grave dug by Taylor and his friends. Nearly twenty years roll by and newspaper items complete the story.

October 1879

In July, 1871, Judge J. C. McClinton, came over to Bodie from Aurora on horseback to look after his Bodie in-terests. While hunting for his horse, who had wandered away, the Judge came across a ridge of loose stones that attracted his attention. During the past summer (1879) some fellow pushed himself into print in connection with the history of Body's grave, etc., in such a manner that the Judge began to smell a lie somewhere and on overhauling his memory con-cluded to go over the ground again.

Hearing of this, Wasson fairly dragged the Judge over the ground and in less than an hour they came upon the identical stone pile. The next day with "Indian Tom", and the necessary tools, they opened the grave of Body. The blanket, in which he was buried, his necktie and shoes were identified as his, and as the evidence was so conclusive furth-er work was suspended until a delegation of reputable citi-zens could be present.

On Monday a party consisting of Hon. F. K. Bechtel, Jos. Wasson, Wm. Irwin, H. B. Davidson, Sheriff-elect James Showers, Geo. Gillson, J. C. Turner, Col. S. W. Blas-del, Warren Loose, Sam Martin, J. T. Baker, of the NEWS, E. R. Cleveland, of the FREE PRESS, and a STANDARD reporter, went out to the half-opened grave. The remains were exhumed and left at Dr. Davidson's office.

It is now right and proper that these remains be given Christian burial and the spot marked by a suitable monu-ment.

Dr. Davidson presented to the Pacific Coast Pioneers at Bodie, the knife and belt that was exhumed with the body of W. S. Body, three days ago. A Committee of Seven members of the Society was appointed to attend the funeral obsequies of Mr. Body, to take place next Sunday afternoon at 3 o'clock from Masonic Hall. The Committee are as follows: Jos. Wasson, Capt. Messic, Dr. Davidson, R. M. Folger, Jerry Lashigh, P. N. Snyder, and Lee McKinstry. Jos. Wasson was appointed to furnish an obituary of Mr. Body, to be spread upon the minutes of the Society, also Mr. R. D. Furguson was selected to deliver an address at the grave.

Next Monday evening a citizens' meeting will be held, having for its object the raising of funds with which to appropriately mark the grave of W. S. Body, it is desired to place a plain slab on the spot where the body was found, and a more elaborate monument in the cemetery where the burial will finally be made.

A Square Funeral. The genuine remains of old man Body were given a very respectable funeral yesterday (Sunday). The afternoon was delightful and the good people of Bodie turned out and gave what was left of the old pioneer, a good, square shakedown. Mr. Ferguson's pithy and pointed address at the grave was a fitting tribute, worthy of the living and the dead. It is now in order to provide a suitable monument over the consecrated spot, in the new cemetery, and also some mark of respect at the spot where the body was found. However much we are now all given to money getting and bread winning, the occasion is one that should not be lost sight of with the burial of this well known pioneer's remains. Let us have no half way measures, but "stand in," and complete the work at once.

November 1879

The Pioneer Society donated $100 to the fund for the Body monument.

During the preparation for the 4th of July celebration in 1881.

A would-be Boothe—an attempt to assassinate the President. Charles Gittau, a Chicago lawyer, the man. The president's prospects of recovering improving. President Garfield was shot before leaving on a limited express at 9:15 this morning.

The Bodie Tunnel

Goodshau Hoisting Works

September 20, 1881

The president is Dead. Hung be the heavens in black, let the sun hide its face from the sight of man. And the moon and stars refuse to show their light while a nation grieves over the untimely loss of its chosen head.

Bodie's tribute September 27 to the memory of James A. Garfield. Bodie honored the memory of the late president, James A. Garfield on Monday in a manner creditable to itself as far as outward performance would indicate, not a thing was left undone.

December 1881

A Good Proposition. There was some talk on the streets Monday in the direction of raising a subscription to buy the monument which was cut a couple of years ago in Bodie and have it erected in the cemetery in honor of the late President Garfield. Why not direct a monument to Bill Bodey—he was the father of this town?

And the fickle public did take and use the monument meant for Bill Bodey and erected it in memory of President Garfield and there it stands today, while in an unmarked grave rests Bill Bodey.

In November of 1878 an editor while not historically correct did write most eloquently:

On Monday last, Gillson and Barber commenced the demolition of the old stone cabin, formerly occupied by W. S. Bodey, the pioneer, whose earthly existence ceased while endeavoring to reach his home through a severe snowstorm during the winter of 1860. In this old tumbledown cabin he passed the dreary months of long winter, with seldom any companion, but an occasional coyote. Years hence, when the pious, now busy tracing the thoughts that teamed through the brain soon to be hushed in death; when the hearts now so full of hopes and ceaseless longings have stopped their beatings; when Mother earth shall have received all that is mortal of thousands now struggling to open hidden treasures being laid bare, will history record the undying faith of the dweller of this old cabin? Of such material are made the pathfinders, whose lot seems to be to live through the storms and hardships of life in order that those who come after may benefit and be blessed by their sacrifices and death.

November 3, 1879, BODIE DAILY FREE PRESS

Bill Body's Bones

Every occasion has a humorous as well as a solemn side . . .
Holding services over the remains of a man that had lain
in the earth for twenty years is of rare occurrence.

Ever since the bones of Body have been unearthed, they
have been the subject of curiosity and comment by nearly
every resident of Bodie. Yesterday afternoon, as they lay in
their miniature coffin, they were closely examined by a
large number of people of all classes. The skull, which had
been carefully cleaned and polished like a billiard ball,
would be taken up and closely scruntinized as if it were a
piece of quartz from some new discovery. At the same time
a lawyer would have the old prospector's shoe, taking it in
from all its bearings. "He must have been a young man," re-
marked an individual dressed in a canvas suit, as he looked
at the row of well preserved teeth. "A man is not like a
horse. You can't tell by his jaw," was the reply of a barkeeper, who had a shin bone in his hand. "He was a man of
firmness," said a carpenter. "You can see that the bump is
very prominent," pointing to the base of the skull, which,
by the way, was a little raised, because of earth adhering and
petrifying. "I knew Body intimately for two years," said an
old-timer from Tuolumne, as he picked up two or three of
his ribs, "and he never drank a drop." "That accounts for the
bones being so well preserved," replied a mine superintendent, who had the left hip bone in his hand looking at it as
if he saw a "color."

Thus the conversation went on, lawyers, doctors, miners,
all examining the remains as though they were a quantity of
good pay ore from the Bodie Mine.

DAILY BODIE STANDARD, October 29, 1879

Judge J. C. McClinton, a past resident of Aurora—Bodie area wrote a letter to the paper:

> The way in which the orthography of Body's name came to be changed . . . was as follows: In 1860, Prof. J. E. Clayton and the Hazlett brothers (Ben and John) located the Bodie Ranch between here and Aurora. They cut the natural growth of grass . . . packed it to Aurora . . . and built a small log stable. They then gave a verbal order for a sign "Body Stable," but the painter, with an eye to the beautiful . . . executed it "Bodie Stable" and the word looked so much better in that form that the people soon adopted that style of spelling it.
>
> I am not now certain to whom we are indebted for this orthographical improvement, but I think it was Robt. M. Howland, who is now in Bodie. At any rate Bob was the first sign painter I remember having seen at Aurora.

On Monday, November 6, 1879 the DAILY FREE PRESS was moved to comment:

> If Bodey had any "git up and git" about him, he would raise up in his newly made grave and make a solemn protest against having his name brought into print so often and spelled in such an outrageous manner.

The miners have a superstition that a sad fate awaits all discoverers. W. S. Bodey died in a snowstorm and never knew that from this find would blossom a town of 10,000 souls and that 90 million dollars would be taken from the town named in his behalf. Several years later E. S. "Black" Taylor (said by some to have been half Cherokee) was a lone occupant of a cabin near Benton and was attacked by hostile Indians. While Taylor fought mightly and killed a reported 10 Indians, he was overpowered and it was rumored that the Indians dismembered him.

Many springs have come and gone, but the Standard still dominates the town as in days of old.

From Bodie Bluff overlooking Bodie.

A. A. Forbes Photo

Assay Office

The Rise and Fall of Bodie

1850's	Placer mining declined on the west slope of the Sierra
1857	Dog Town—Mormons found gold
1859	Washoe excitement, the Comstock at Virginia City—impetus for movement to the east side of the Sierra—silver ore with gold—lasted through 60's and '70's
1859	Monoville—gold
1859	W. S. Bodey and mining companions found gold north of Mono Lake
1859-60	Winter W. S. Bodey perished in snowstorm
1860	Bodey, Body or Bodie Mining District organized
1860	Esmeralda excitement (produced town of Aurora) detracted attention from the Bodie diggings
1860's	Benton — silver — 1864 Montgomery Mining District formed
1860's	Cerro Gordo—silver and lead
1861	Bunker Hill Mine located, later to become the Standard Mining Company
1861	Oldest building in Bodie—now known as Hydro Building
1863	Bodie Bluff Consolidated Mining Company—first mining corporation formed
1874-76	Panamint—Silver
1877	Mammoth—silver and gold ore discovered
1874	Essington and Lockwood have cave in that exposes rich gold ore that in time makes the Standard famous
1878	Bodie Mining Company makes phenomenally rich strike of gold and silver ore—the rush is on in earnest. Bodie stock jumped from fifty cents to fifty-four dollars a share
1878-1879	Most terrible winter in the history of Bodie

1879	Lundy—gold discovered—Homer Mining District
1879	Bodey's bones are given elaborate funeral and placed in Bodie cemetery
1879-1880	Pinnacle of production
1879-1881	Bodie population reached between 10,000 and 13,000
X Late 1880's	Bodie experienced first decline
1881	Bodie Railway and Lumber Co. formed to haul wood, lumber from Mono Mills to the town of Bodie
X1881	Was apparent that the Standard and the Bodie had been the only profitable mines
1881	Stock market went to pieces
1886	First fire
X1887	Standard and Bodie mines merged and operated successfully for 20 years
1892	July 25, 1892—Bodie experienced disastrous fire
1892	World's first hydro-electric power transmission—from Green Creek to the Standard Con. at Bodie
1895	New cyanide process successfully used in Bodie—Bodie boomed again
1910	Hydro Electro Plant at Jordan turns on electricity for power and lights in Bodie proper
1911	Avalanche brings death and destruction to Hydro Electro Plant at Jordan
1912	Steady decline of Bodie
1915	Mines declined, many closed

Courtesy of William Glenn

18-horse team hauling generator through the streets of Bodie.

1917	Bodie railroad abandoned
1920's	Exploratory work
1932	June 23, 1932—Fire again destroys the majority of buildings in Bodie
1938-1941	Gold recovery activity
1962	Bodie becomes a State Historic Park under the California State Division of Beaches and Parks
1964	September 12, 1964—dedication of Bodie as a California Historic Site—Bodie is also a National Historic Site

Tioga Mine

From Grant Smith's "Bodie: Last of the Old-Time Mining Camps" came this description of John Wagner's saloon.

". . . I do not know how many men were killed in John Wagner's saloon. That was a typical mining camp saloon, somewhat larger than any of the others. It was a barn-like room, fronting on the main street; probably 30 ft. wide, 100 ft. long, and 15 ft. high. To the left of the swinging-doors, as you entered, was the bar, stretched along the side of the room. Opposite the bar, and stretching along in similar fashion, was a chop-house, or short-order restaurant, with a long counter and stools in front. The rear of the room was literally filled with gambling-tables of one kind and another, principally faro-banks, presided over by silent, watchful dealers, with hundreds, or even thousands, of dollars in gold and silver stacked up in front of them, and a gun always within reach."

THE RISE AND FALL OF BODIE...

Personal observations of correspondents and of the reporters of the newspapers paints for us a picture of the rise and fall of Bodie.

In 1861 a correspondent writes:

> There are three quartz mills in the county, two in the Bodie district driven by steam, and one at Hot Springs driven by water. The former carry, the one 16, and the other 12 stamps, and the latter four. The entire cost of these mills has been about $200,000.

Another report in 1863 predicts:

> Gold and silver mines of undoubted value exist in Bodie mining district, a few miles west of Aurora, and that locality will probably be the center of considerable population at no distant day.

November 1877

> Bodie presents a very lively appearance, but you are to assure your readers that there are more men here at present than can procure work. They had better wait until spring, when there will be plenty of openings. The camp can not be said to be overdone, but it will be if there are any more crowding in. There are three general merchandising houses, a dozen saloons, six restaurants, one tin shop, one shoemaker, and other businesses are represented. The mines are all looking well, and the camp has a bright future. Everybody is preparing for a hard winter; wood is high and hard to get. Had a shooting scrape last night, but no damage was done, a Mexican got off with a flesher. They tell me they have select fights about every night, but with the exception of a few discolored objects, which the owners say was caused by falling down, no one would suppose that there is anything to mar the peaceful quietness of the town.

December 1877

> Lively times in Bodie: Main Street has presented a lively sight during the past week. The weather has been all that could be asked for, and out of door work has been pushed in every direction. The stores, shops and saloons have been doing a big trade, especially in the last five days, with nearly $70,000 in miner's wages circulating around. Wagons, long trains and stages arriving daily with freight and passengers; interested crowds eagerly discussing the latest strike, or some new discovery; capitalists and prospectors joining forces or driving quick, business-like bargains; the rush and stir of the superintendents hurrying their winter supplies to safe

A. A. Forbes Photo

Courtesy of Los Angeles County Museum

Bodie, Calif. 8367

A.A.Forbes Photo

and convenient shelter while the favorable weather lasts; all these are the sights and sounds of a prosperous growing mining town, on a solid substantial basis.

February 1878

Bodie bids fair to be one of the loudest camps on the coast next summer. The town of Bodie is situated on a flat, said to be 2,000 feet higher than Mt. Davidson. God knows it is high enough for me. The flat is about two miles in length by a half a mile in width, and contains less than 175 or 180 houses and cabins. All classes of business is represented. We have hotels, restaurants, stores of all kinds, blacksmith shops, tailor shops, jewelry shops and plenty of whisky mills and other mills that will not be mentioned. Tell all who talk of coming to Bodie to speculate without money, to stay home, as the place is overrun with men seeking employment; in addition to that, nothing but coin buys grub here—check will not do.

February 1878

Bodie has a population of 1500 people, about 600 of whom are out of employment, and which number not only 250 would work could they find it to do. There are in the town 17 saloons, five stores, two livery stables, 6 restaurants, one newspaper, 4 barber shops, two butcher shops, one fruit

Panoramic view of Main Street, Bodie before the 1932 fire.

store, board and lodging houses, two boot shops, one tin shop, one jewelry shop, one saddle shop, two drug stores, three doctors, four lawyers, post office, express office, 15 houses of ill fame, one bakery, two lumber yards, two daily stage lines, and the usual secret societies and a Miner's Union. Lots are worth from $100 to $1000. Lumber sells at $70 to $100 per thousand. There are six or seven good mines and about 700 locations for mines. Of course, nearly everyday there are new locations made. There are two 20-stamp mills which turn out about $40,000 each month. The average number of arrivals each day is 10. In the spring everybody looks for lively times in Bodie. The roads south of Carson are not bad as one might expect, yet no one would care to drive over them were he on a pleasure trip. Many persons in Bodie are elated over the prospects of the camp, while others speaking of it use language wholly unbecoming a Christian. Those who have money and desire to go into business here, may just as well come now, perhaps it would be better than to wait until summer. What may be the result of this new mining excitement, of course, none can tell. There will be, beyond doubt, a great many disappointed people; a few will make a strike, few, a very few, perhaps, a fortune.

Courtesy of Death Valley Museum

University and Maryland Mines

July 1878

There are 27 saloons in Bodie and it is estimated that there are over 1700 drinks taken every day over the bars. The amount taken by any one man would undoubtedly make his friends think he was slightly off.

August 1878

Bodie is honored with no less than thirteen law firms.

The streets of the city present a very animated appearance these days.

October 1878

There are now 19 steam hoisting works in Bodie, and several more on the road. There will be 25 mines worked all winter by steam, which will insure a pretty lively camp.

December 1878, GRASS VALLEY UNION

Bodie has a population of 5,000, including the suburb around the Bodie and Standard Mines. The Main Street is nearly one mile long and lots are staked off in all directions on the hillsides. Buildings grow as if by magic, and the resident of Bodie who absents himself for a week or two on a trip to the Bay, returns and views with surprise the buildings erected during his absence. The growth of the town has no parallel in the history of mining. Average arrivals are about 30, and all departees intend to return. Society has not assimilated, but the elements exist in a state of chaos. Fine residences, saloons, business houses, brothels and cabins are in a motley jumble as to location. There are 47 saloons and ten faro tables. This is not a disparagement of the district, but an evidence of its prosperity.

There are however two banking houses, five wholesale stores, and an excellent daily newspaper, and all the accessories of civilization and refinement will soon follow. The slow and healthy growth of the town was accelerated during the present year by the extraordinary development of Bodie Consolidated Mine, which paid its stockholders $600,000 in dividends during a career of less than six months. The Standard dividends aggregate $800,000 and the company possesses about $200,000 in supplies and machinery.

The bullion product is only limited by the milling facilities. There are at present in Bodie only four mills: the Standard, 20 stamps; the Syndicate, 20 stamps, running on Bodie ores; the Bodie, 10 stamps, running on Bodie tailings; the Miners, a custom mill, five stamps. Early in the spring the Bulwer will erect a 20 stamp mill and the Standard will increase its facilities. It is safe to predict the bullion

Jupiter Hoisting Works

product for 1879 will average $1,000,000 per month for ten months of the year. There will be at least five dividend paying mines: The Standard, Bodie, Bulwer—but those who are good at "guessing" may select the other two.

Articles were sent back to the RENO WEEKLY GAZETTE by the correspondent Honest Miner on his trip to Bodie and tell of his experiences while there.

June 15, 1879

A great deal of freight goes over the road. (Talking about his trip into Bodie) Wheeler and Co. have 20 horse teams which leave Carson daily making the trip in three days hauling 40,000 to 45,000 pounds. The toll is $28.00 per team for the round trip. They go north with empty wagons . . . Aurora is what Bob Burns would call "a good old has been." It is surrounded and filled with ruins and broken walls. The foundations of old hoisting works, quartz mills are thicker than statesmen in congress . . . The Syndicate, Bodie and Miners Mills hammer away a couple of miles from town . . .

June 17, 1879—Honest Miner

LABOR MARKET. Bodie crowded with men of every trade looking for work.

Prospects of the Town. The streets of Bodie are crowded with men. A fight or a fiddle will draw hundreds of heads together and render the passage of teams slow and difficult. Every stage coming in is loaded. Men are flocking in on the Sonora Road on foot, on horseback and in wagon. They are nearly all looking for work, and not one in five has money enough to live on for a week. The population of Bodie is now between four and five thousand, and there is work for about 800. The way the idlers manage to get grub is one of the tricks of the trade. They "strike" everyone they have ever seen, as often as they can possibly expect to get a cent. One man who has been here a week, tells me he has given away 12 dollars to hungry men. He is a mechanic and a poor man. They sleep in chairs until the saloons close up, and then walk the streets until morning. They pick up "sleepers" on the faro tables, and when permitted to do so, turn sleepers on the same tables when the game is over. An early riser will see them crawling out, stiff and shivering, yawning and stretching. Men are frequently garroted and robbed by them, sneak thieves are constantly plying their trade. Intelligent working men tell me that there are today, five mechanics to one job, three laborers to one job, two miners to one job. There are hosts of gamblers, and a great number of men who would not work under any circumstances, in addition to those who really want work and can not get it. Men who are thinking of coming to this country in search of work should consider that there is a vast difference between gold and silver mines, in regard to the amount of labor required to work them . . .

I only know one place where the climate is likely to be more disagreeable, and that is the sulphury regions, where we are informed on good authority, that there is weeping and wailing and gnashing of teeth. There is plenty of gnashing of teeth here, not only early in the morning, but at all times of the day when it is cloudy or windy. There is hardly a day in the year without ice on all the standing water in the neighborhood, and one day I walked across a little pond, on the ice. The men at work on the hill putting up machinery had to quit work on account of a snowstorm a week ago and did not do a stroke of work for a day and a half.

June 18, 1879—Honest Miner

Mining towns persist in locating themselves right up

The Bodie Stage (run by Cecil Burkham) in Bodie Canyon enroute to Aurora.
A. A. Forbes Photo   Los Angeles County Museum and Cecil Burkham

against the dump piles instead of choosing a favorable site, and occupying it with something like a common regard for order and fitness. It would be much better for the miners if they were separated even by a little distance from the whiskey mills and gambling hells that lie in wait for them, but such a town will never be built. This little city is strung along the Sonora and Aurora road like an elongated banana on a cord. The fact that the road ran along on a marshy bank of a little creek has no influence on the selection of location. Nor did the winding of the stream and the crowding in of the hills on either side, which makes a bend necessary on the main street in the center of town. If it has gone just its own length further south and put the north end where the south end now rests, it would have been on a very handsome ground. This place which is a grassy level plot was very marshy before the Standard drained it to get water for the mill. Outside of Main Street there are scattered houses on the hill and to the east, reaching to the foot of Bodie Bluffs, and quite a street on the hillside west of town. This street is composed of little two and three room wooden houses uniform size, where the Magdalenes reside. The town is built of pine, much of it of heavy pitchy stuff from Bridgeport country . . . Everyone expecting a fire—the only preparations being made to fight fire is a Babcock engine and a hook and ladder company.

Sleigh in Bodie Canyon.

Courtesy of McDonell sisters

The Oddfellows and Masons each have a lodge and a chapter and a Commandery is being organized. Masonic Hall is about ready for work. Miners Union counts 500 members. There is a good school building, but no church, although the Methodists and Catholics each have been served the guidance of regular parsons. There are two solid banks, some very large stores and a going lot of saloons: some of them very elegant ones. The elevation of Bodie can not be much over 8400 feet.

The climate of Bodie seems to be very unhealthy especially for men. Yet there are over 300 children here and they seem to enjoy the best of health. Ladies also are seldom sick. In 15 months only 4 women and 1 child have been buried, while for many weeks there has been a funeral every day. The enemy is pneumonia which attacks the strongest men in preference to the sickly or the weak. The air is light and cold, the men who become overheated are chilled almost instantly, unless extraordinary precautions are taken and their lungs have to bear the whole shock. Living here is very cheap in comparison. Transient customers pay 50 cents a meal at a chop house, similar to those popular at Virginia City. A good room costs a dollar a night.

June 26, 1879—Honest Miner tells about a guided tour through the Bodie Mine. He explains their descent down the shaft and then continues:

This streak is about 18 inches wide, and underneath it lies an inch and a half of gold, with hardly enough rock to color it. Much of the rock is finely powdered and crumbles in the hand, and yet is held together so closely by the matted gold that it can hardly be pulled apart with the fingers . . . Here it contains horn silver and much gold. The wonderful richness of this streak of ore, which goes all through the Bodie, and which has been cut into at different places, may be judged by the fact that in the mill, after a 24 hour's run, the dies got so clogged up with gold that the stamps could not play. Crow bars were sharpened and used as cold chisels, and 168 pounds were dug out and put into a bag, which is kept in the office for visitors to lift.

Personal experiences of an old Bodieite published on December 4, 1909 tells of his experiences in 1878 when the gold stopped the 30 stamp mill.

In one day's run that I can remember we got out about 200 pounds of gold amalgamate. I have had the gold accumulate in the battery until I recognized by the sound that the stamps were no longer crushing rock and that they were not striking iron. I would take off the screen and find that the gold had accumulated on the mortar until it was flush with the dies and I would have to take out a single mortar with an ordinary iron shovel such as we use for cleaning up free gold. Enough to fill Wells Fargo Express boxes. Eighty pounds amalgamate from one charge in the pan was a very usual thing during the run of the ore. We were obliged to retort during the whole time as rapidly as the retorts cooled and a fresh charge of amalgamate could be put into it. During the run of the ore, Peter Holmes, Bob Vixon (?) and myself went into the mines. Before going we stopped at one of the stores and got ordinary 5 pound shot bags to take with us as sample sacks. We filled this bag with loose dirt scraped from the face of the drifts with our hands. From this we panned out in Peter Holmes' house after this enough gold to make our match boxes. Any miner can understand what that means.

November 20, 1879, RENO WEEKLY GAZETTE

A Trip to Bodie. L. P. Walker recently returned from a trip to Bodie and Aurora.

Business is very prosperous and the merchants are kept busy. Stocks are good and are kept on hand. Gilson Co. have a stock of merchandise valued at 180,000 dollars and there are four or five other concerns that carry stocks each worth $100,000. A small hotel with about 20 rooms, called the Mono House, rents for $800.00 a month.

The reports about pneumonia in Bodie have been much exaggerated. The victims to the disease are commonly men who get drunk and lie about the streets or those who expose themselves to sudden chills. With proper precautions no one need fear pneumonia. Mr. Walker desires to warn everyone going to Bodie against the fatal effects of drinking whiskey. The fumes of the whiskey, he thinks, combined with the rarity of the air or the low temperature and/or dust, or mingle with the elevation and the ozone, or somehow in a way that owing to the extreme dryness of the atmosphere may be perhaps be mitigated, it is still apt to produce a degree of mental exhileration that should be or at least is in great part due to peculiar climatic conditions that surround, so to speak, in a region the somewhat anomalous state of the site of low civilization of the camp.

The last sentence could be used as a sobriety test for those affected by the "fumes of whiskey."

The need of a church is becoming more and more urgent everyday, and Mr. Walker took a great interest in the efforts that are being made to establish a place of worship for the devout of Bodie. He called upon several acting clergymen of the place and was told that the deaths from pneumonia was producing a beneficial effect in the way of directing the inhabitants toward the consideration of the probability of the hereafter.

October, November and December 1880

A large number of Chinamen have left town during the past few weeks. This change is noticeable from the presence of vacant washhouses and apparent desertion of the Chinese quarters.

A Deserted Quarter—The north end of Main Street is growing more deserted and dreary everyday. Anytime— three years ago—that section was a flouishing part of Bodie, but the town has moved up and left it demoralized. The signs for rent and for sale are frequent, and the houses are falling into decay. What were at one time handsome saloons are now old shells, covered with cobwebs, dust and gloom. Mining camps go up canyons invariably and this is one reason why the north end is now deserted and uninviting. At present time a lean and hungry coyote can wander through the backyards unmolested, and the tarantula and the bats dance

FIRE! Fire was the scourge of all early-day wooden western mining towns. Fire was feared and precautions were taken by maintaining a hose cart and a fire house and installing water lines. The fire bell also proclaimed the news and events. The fire bell clanged with great insistency when there was a fire but when there was a funeral procession wending its way up the hill to the cemetery, the bell tolled slowly.

to their favorite music in the old saloons. When Bodie booms again, all these things will change, and the hand of prosperity will touch the "north end" and make it flouish like a family of white mice.

Hard Times—These are perilous times. And the master who can keep his vessel off the rocks is indeed fortunate. Saloons are transitory. In the morning they are opened with a great flourish, free drinks and a full house. In the evening the handsome front is spotted over with decorations furnished by the sheriff. The proprietor goeth his way and the place knowth him no more.

The courts are deserted these days, and the attorneys have time to read the latest Supreme court decisions.

Off for Utah—Several miners have left here for Utah during the past few days. Carpenters are complaining for the scarcity of work. Real estate is at a standstill. It is hard to sell property at the present time. Dance halls are now running to poor music and poor money. The justice courts are dull and inactive. Lawyer's fees are few and far between. Lower Main Street is in deplorable condition.

January to June 1881

Stage robberies every two or three days seems to be the occupation of the unemployed.

June 1881

The population of Bodie is smaller at present than at any time since the first strike in Bodie Con.

Could it be that the old mining camp prophecy proved true in Bodie?

"A hanging and a church will kill any camp."

The S. G. Albright team after it had unloaded 30,000 pounds of machinery at the Standard Mill Co. after hauling it from Carson City, Nevada in 1894.
Courtesy of Mrs. Floris E. Harris

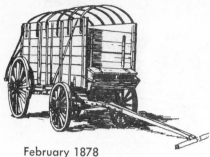

February 1878

There are three daily stages between here and Aurora and one daily to Bridgeport.

August 1878

The Sonora Stage Line is doing a good business. The arrivals exceed the departures two to one.

October 1878

Two lines of six-horse coaches, with extra daily on the Carson route, come in filled with passengers from deck to keelson. Sixteen is an average load.

Wells Fargo Express charges one percent for express charges on all bullion shipments from Bodie to San Francisco. The company insures the bullion against robbers, provides a guard of 7 armed men and it renumerates the stage company for the loss of passenger traffic on the days that the bullion is sent. No passengers travel on the stage with the bullion.

We do know that Bodie ore is being constantly hauled through our streets by 16-mule teams, and that Squire Hildreth, at the Standard Mill, is kept busy melting and refining the bullion.

Today Main Street was almost blocked up with heavy freight teams loaded with merchandise from below. We are informed that these arrivals are only the advance guard

Panoramic view of Bodie from the cemetery on the hill. The townspeople passed judgement to determine who would be buried inside the fence with the respectable citizens and who would be placed outside the fenced area in boot hill with what they considered to be the lawless and sinful element.

Freight Lines

of a long string now enroute from all sections of the country.

BODIE WEEKLY STANDARD

October 23, 1878

A Big Team. Smith, the champion single line teamster, arrived in town today from Carson, with a load of lumber, etc., weighing upwards of 40,000 pounds. This immense load was hauled by 16 fine looking mules, all of which made a display such as seldom seen in any camp.

November 1878

George Elder, the man who owns 13 of the finest 18-mule teams on the coast, came to Bodie Monday evening. He says he has within the past few days, t a k e n 200,000 pounds of freight from the depot at Carson, for Bodie, without making a perceptible hole in the pile.

January 1879

A new stage line, owned by John Alman, to run between Bodie and the Comstock by the way of Aurora and Mason Valley, will commence sometime this month and the service will be tri-weekly.

April 1880

The stages come in loaded with passengers and go out loaded with bullion.

CHRONICLE UNION

August 1880

Sage brush is placed on the Bodie-Big Meadows Road to keep the dust down.

1881

A fly wheel weighing 8½ tons was shipped on a special truck, drawn by sixteen mules, from Carson to Bodie for the Noonday Mine.

Courtesy of Death Valley Museum

THE BODIE EVENING MINER
Tuesday, February 12, 1884

William Fairfield has a young man engaged snowshoeing the Bridgeport letter mail in and out of Bodie, He is only fifty-seven years of age, and his name is J. C. McTarnahan. Mc. says he knows but little about the science of snow-shoeing but thinks success lies, mainly, in the power continuance. He and McAlpin left at eight o'clock this morning for Bridgeport on Norwegians.

Monday, February 18, 1884

S. B. Burkham arrived with his team from Lundy Saturday, but had to return on snowshoes today.

Monday, February 25, 1884

Stage Drivers—Most anybody can be a stage driver in summer time, but it takes a man of iron constitution for the winters, such as we are having this year. Con Denise and H. A. Billings have been shoveling snow, changing horses from coach to sleigh, working night and day, and having a tough time generally on the short route from Hawthorne to Bodie. They are at present running coach only as far as Gus Aaroe's station where they change to sleigh and run into Bodie on runners.

Charlie and Mildred McMillan out for a sleigh ride in Bodie.

The Hawthorne Stage owned by Cecil Burkham takes to sleigh during the w i n t e r months.
Courtesy of Cecil Burkham

Courtesy of William Glenn

Three stages in readiness to travel: first, Charlie Fulton of Mono Lake-Bodie Stage; second, Art Murphy and Will Bell on the Bridgeport-Bodie Stage run; third, Oscar Snyder, driver of the Hawthorne-Bodie Stage.

A ten-horse team moves down Main Street in Bodie. The McDonell sisters remember the lovely sound of the bells on the freight teams. They could recognize by the sound of the bells whether the approaching team was of their uncle's, James Duncan Welsh, or those of the Allen or Conway teams.

A. A. Forbes Photo   **Cecil Burkham and Los Angeles County Museum**

Stage Coach in front of the Grand Hotel. Photo taken in 1880. Driver of the six horse team is "Big" Tom Petit. Beside him is old Wardy, Wells Fargo messenger, holding sawed-off shot gun. Driver of four horse team is George Finney. Back of him, with arms akimbo, is Charles Daniels. Gentleman leaning on balcony at left is Samuel Southworth. The lady is Mrs. Chestnut, landlady of the hotel. I. Stoddard Penfield is standing at head of white horse. The Grand Central Hotel was not of adobe, but a frame structure, two stories in height. The lower floor on one side was a stage office, on the other a wide bar, back of which were the usual gambling games. The upper floors were made into bedrooms by partition of studding. Over this was tacked cotton cloth and then wall paper.

The Bodie Pioneer Stage Line Office was located at 3 Montgomery Street, San Francisco shown here in photo taken in 1880. An old ad states that the fare from San Francisco to Bodie to be $36.00 and the time for the trip to take 36 hours.

Four-mule team, Bodie-Hawthorne Stage, Oscar Snyder on left, Will Bell on right.

Friday, March 7, 1884

Staging—Yesterday the Hawthorne stage got to just below Hank Blanchard's from half past eight o'clock in the morning until two o'clock in the afternoon. They were four hours going four hundred yards. The snow full of water and the horses almost out of sight at times. Driver and helpers up to their waists in water part of the time.

Wednesday, March 19, 1884

Mike Tovey guarded $25,000 worth of bullion out of town today— $10,700.98 from the Standard Con., and $13,658.61 from the Little Pet, or Bodie Con.

Thursday, March 20, 1884

News item: H. P. Noyes and N. J. Wilson came in on snowshoes yesterday from Summers' ranch, near the Detroit copper works, arriving in Bodie at eleven o'clock last night. They brought a horse and sleigh with them to take back a supply of provisions. The animal had on snowshoes made of two inch plank twelve inches square, being fastened to his feet by means of steel clasps made to fit the hoof. Mr. Wilson had one of his feet badly frozen.

Monday, March 31, 1884

Hector has a tandem team attached to his stage bob sleigh. Each of the two animals wear four snow shoes, ten inches square made of rubber belting. His return load Saturday was principally potatoes from the Italians' ranch. No passenger traffic these days.

Thursday, April 10, 1884

Last evening Ed Hector abandoned his Lundy stage sleigh down in the canyon; one of the animals led the procession into Bodie with the mailbags on his back and a rope hitched to his tail. At the other end of the rope was Ed acting as engineer although the way in which he hung back on the rope would indicate that he was being assisted into town. The other animals brought up the rear, acting as a push engine.

Saturday, May 3, 1884

HANK MARTIN'S VICISSITUDES

Hank Martin was on his way to Darwin with three strings of wagons, two wagons in a string, one four horse commissary wagon loaded with grub, a Chinese frypan manipulator, blankets for twelve men, two horse spring wagon for the bosses to ride in, and sixty-three animals and twelve men. After struggling hard through the deep snow on Goat Ranch Hill for three days, the entire outfit went back by way of Bridgeport and Sweetwater, thence by way of Fletcher's and Belleville. This experiment of road breaking must have cost a cool five hundred. Sixty-three animals and twelve men are a small circus in themselves, and it cost money to feed them all and pay wages to the men.

INYO REGISTER

May 27, 1886

Teaming. E. W. Fleniken makes regular semi-monthly trips to Bodie with loads of eggs, butter, and all kinds of farm produce, most of his supply being obtained from Bulpitt and Meroney.

INYO REGISTER

December 16, 1886

Round Valley Letter

Teaming—To Mono Mills and Bodie has been lively this fall. Considerable Round Valley produce—chickens, eggs, honey, turkeys, butter, pork, feed, flour, etc.—finds a good

Cat and sled hauling mining timbers to Bodie.

Standard hoisting works and lumber shed.

market in that direction. The many big dollars received from there are very acceptable. We expect to see friend Sherwin connect the Bodie railroad (which he says Supt. Holt must run through this valley) with the C. & C. All the women are anxious to see the railroad extended southward to salt water, etc.

BODIE MINER
January 23, 1909

Johnny Yribarren has a terrible experience. Gets lost in a snow storm and has a narrow escape from death.

Out in a wild storm, with the wind blowing a hurricane, all sense of direction lost, entirely beyond the reach of assistance and having to keep moving to prevent freezing,

is experience of John Yribarren, the mail contractor between Bodie and Lundy.

Thursday morning he left Mono Lake on scheduled time and without serious trouble reached Cottonwood Canyon about 5 o'clock in the evening. After leaving the place, a period of storm increased, the drifts deepened, the familiar landmarks disappeared in the shroud of snow with the coming of darkness. Bravely the tired horses fought their way through the gigantic drifts until exhausted and worn out, they gave up the struggle. Mr. Yribarren tramped around in the snow in an effort to find the road but his efforts were useless and, disheartened and discouraged, he devoted

W. E. Reading Store—note snow tunnel to store entrance at street level.

Main Street of Bodie in 1912 with Post Office entrance at right edge of picture.

the remainder of the night to exercising and keeping from freezing to death.

After the tramping and shouting throughout what seemed to him an endless night, a portion of which time he was delirious, Yribarren discovered at daylight that he was near the summit, and about two miles from Bodie, and about two hundred yards from a cabin, known as Seiler's, where he could have spent the night in comparative comfort. He walked into Bodie, arriving here in an exhausted condition. His wants were attended to and his team was sent after. One of the horses, a valuable animal, died this morning, supposedly from strain and exposure. Mr. Yribarren is around town today, but he is feeling the results of the terrible experience, and says he desires no more of the kind.

Oct. 16, 1909

Bodie Stage Is Overturned — The Hawthorne-Bodie up stage Thursday met with an accident at Lucky Boy which came near being a serious proposition. As it is, Frank Williams the driver, is laid up with a badly lacerated scalp, 33 stitches being taken in it alone. One Lucky Boy, Frank, went to the Mocha restaurant to buy some bread for Summit Station. He climbed in and onto the stage and picked up his lines to start. One of the leaders switched his tail, caught the lines and immediately started down the hill. The tongue was broken out of the stage, the vehicle overturned, the driver thrown against a rock on the upper hillside. Medical attention was secured for Mr. Williams by J. T. Bryson, secured the rig and brought in the mail and the passengers. Cecil Burkham went down yesterday and will bring Mr. Williams if he is able to travel to Bodie.

Feb. 1909

Bodie, Mono Lake and Lundy Stage Co. John Yribarren, propriator leaves Bodie Monday at 6 o'clock, reurns from Lundy in the afternoon. Arrives in Bodie at 7 o'clock. Fare to Lundy — $4. Fare to Lundy and return — $7. Fare to Mono Lake — $3. Freight — Bodie to Lundy — or Lundy to Bodie — 1½ cents per pound. Freight Bodie to Mono Lake or Mono Lake to Bodie— 1 cent per pound. No package to take for less than 25 cents.

By this time automobiles had replaced horses on the Burkham stages.

Courtesy of William Glenn

The Pope and Thomas Flyer were the popular cars of the day.

Mail arriving at Bodie, 1912. Cecil Burkham, stage owner and operator.

Relics of Bodie's past—when horsepower was used for fun, for work or
for transportation to the last resting
place.
Courtesy Mono County Museum

Distance from Carson to Bodie:

Carson to 12-Mile House .... 19.2 miles
12-Mile House to Carter's 7.3
Carter's to Mountain House 7.5
Mountain House to Wellington 12.7
Wellington to Sulphur 12.5
Sulphur to Sweetwater .... 12.
Sweetwater to Elbow 9.6
Elbow to Fletcher 9.1
Fletcher to Del Monte 6
Del Monte to Sunshine .... 3.
Sunshine to Bodie .... 7.

Ruins of the Sunshine Stage Station near Bodie (see mileage chart above). Old watering
trough is in center foreground. Sunshine Station was located between Bodie and the
California-Nevada state line.
Courtesy of California Historical Society

WOOD

Jupiter Hoisting Works

November 1877

The great cry in Bodie just now is "WOOD." Everybody is preparing for a hard winter; wood is high and hard to get.

January 1878

Over one-third of Bodie's orders on Carson for lumber will remain unfilled until next spring. The number of buildings here now would be increased by as many again if there was the lumber here to supply the demand at any price.

Over 40,000 feet of lumber is daily expected in Bodie from Reno. The prices fixed at some $85 to $110 per thousand.

June 1878

Ben F. Butler, who contracted with the Standard Company to deliver 7,000 cords of wood between April and November, has sublet the contract to Mr. Elders, who will proceed to packing and hauling same, delivering 70 cords daily. There are 150 mules now used packing wood to the camp. The contract price is $8.12½ per cord.

Mr. Bowman has a contract for furnishing 2,000 cords of wood for the Syndicate Mill. It will be necessary that he pack the wood 2½ miles and then haul it 5 miles.

August 1878

Bids are asked for 1000 cords of nut pine wood to be delivered at the Bechtel mine before October 30.

The Standard's big wood pile continues to grow.

October 1878

Hank Blanchard tells us that there are nearly 50,000 feet of clear lumber now on the way here from Carson City.

There are now 19 steam hoisting works in Bodie, and several more on the road. There will be about 25 mines worked all winter by steam, which will insure a pretty lively camp.

Courtesy Mono County Museum

Bodietes remember hearing the sing-song chant of the wood cutters as they herded their wood trains into town. Here a typical Chinese wood train enters town on the Aurora road.

Burro train unloading wood at the Red Cloud Mine. In later years a narrow gauge track was built to run in front of the boilers. The cordwood was thrown from the cars directly into the boilers—some Bodietes estimate that there were 50 boilers at the Red Cloud. Later these boilers were utilized as pipe at Mill Creek at the Lundy Dam.

A. A. Forbes Photo   Courtesy of C. Lorin Ray

November 1878

The Bridgeport sawmill is now prepared to furnish lumber at $45 per thousand.

BODIE WEEKLY STANDARD
December 4, 1878

Wood pirates beware! Some night, when the storm beats against their piratical cabins, there will be an explosion, and the wood piles that knew them once will know them no more. We will be prepared to receive your next visit, Mr. Wood Pirate, i n the manner once the boast of people, with bloody hands to a hospitable grave. We mean business.

December 1878

Bang. There has been a rise in wood. A man living in the south end of town took a stick of wood lying handy on a neighbor's pile. It burnt very well until the giant powder cartridge in the end of the wood went off. The stove and a section of the roof went with it. The wicked neighbor laughed in his sleep.

December 11, 1878

There are now many thousands of feet on hand in the yards and more arriving daily which will be increased from time to time as the demand requires. The great rush is now over and those contemplating building either have lumber engaged or will wait until spring. We must say right here that the faithful fulfillments, promises on the part of Mr. Hunnewill has done much to relieve the deadlock which at one time seemed imminent both as it reflects our town and the mines.

September 1879

The demand for lumber continues to be unprecedented and it is still with only great effort the dealers can keep up with the demand.

Packing wood into Bodie with the Occidental Hotel in the background.

Courtesy Mono County Museum

PACKING WOOD BODIE CAL.

Tremendous pile of wood in the back of the Standard. Woodpile is in the center of a triangle formed by the Standard on the left, the mule barns on the top right and the house of Theodore Hoover (President Herbert Hoover's brother), center right.

Winter's Wood. There is now cut and piled in various districts contingent to Bodie, over 18,500 cords of wood.

Spring 1880
Wood is selling at $18 to $20 per cord, and a short measure at that, this is extortion pure and simple.

CHRONICLE UNION, May 29, 1880
Eagle Sawmill—Buckeye Canyon, 10 team loads 10,000 square feet lumber for Bodie.

BODIE WEEKLY STANDARD,
Newspaper quote—Nov. 23, 1895
The wood traffic—Our wood dealers are making the most of the present fine weather to fill their wood contracts, and the wood piles are growing to a goodly portion all over town. The piutes will find no scarcity of work this winter for "hogadie" — wood dealers can be seen at all hours of the day passing through our streets with the indispensable article of domestic use.

SOME ACTION NEEDED
1880

The present severe storm (April 21) should admonish all that, unless immediate steps are taken in regard to the fire wood question, there will be much distress among the poor. A man should be lightly punished, if at all, for stealing firewood in such a climate as we have in Bodie when $25 per cord is demanded for it. We suppose, however, that the demand is legitimate, as anything seems to be with a good

Burros packing wood in the snow.
Courtesy of McDonell sisters

William Young reminisces, "There was an old inactive Cornish Pump at the Bodie Mine when I came to Bodie in 1910. Had a big walking beam with the weight on one side to balance the water. This one was at the end of the forward stroke and someone had taken off the lid of the steam chest—where the steam was admitted to the cylinder. It was so large that I could crawl right down through those valves into the piston. The piston was about 6 feet and had a stroke of about 5 or 6 feet. It didn't rotate, you know, it just went back and forth. The piston rod was 6 inches in diameter and tapered out to about 12 inches and back to the other end—it was a stretched out diamond shape. It hooked on to the walking beam that rocked the sucker rods on the pump."

many people here. A public meeting to consider the question and devise some plan to increase the wood supply should be held at once.

The severest wind and snow storm of the season is that which has prevailed since yesterday morning. (April 22).

The people as well as most of the mines of Bodie are out of fire wood, and unless some action is taken at once there will be suffering in town. Several mines have been compelled to shut down for lack of wood with which to run their hoisting works, and several others will be compelled to stop unless, within a few days, the road to the wood "ranches" can be opened.

We have had snow storms for the past seven months, and still they come.

THE WOOD FAMINE BROKEN

The wood famine, which presented such a serious aspect ten days ago, has been broken by the opening of the Standard wood road to the wood ranches, south of Mono Lake. This work was effected by popular subscription.

Fire wood has fallen from thirty to twelve dollars per cord.

Bodie Railway

February 18, 1881—Bodie Railway and Lumber Co. was organized

November 8, 1881—First train whistle heard in Bodie

November 14, 1881—Last spike driven

1882—Changed name to Bodie and Benton Railway and Commercial Co.

1893—Regained title of Bodie Railway and Lumber Co.

December 23, 1906—Mono Lake Railway and Lumber Co.

1908—Mono Railway Co. and Mono Lake Lumber Co. The lumber and railroad interests were separated

September 6, 1917—Abandoned

1918—Sold for scrap iron

When the rails and equipment of the railroad were sold in 1918, Supt. Emil W. Billeb was in charge of taking up the rails and delivering the equipment to Benton, California.

Bodie Railway and Lumber Company train.
Courtesy of Bancroft Library

On the Bodie railroad in 1910.
Courtesy Nevada State Museum

Lime was produced at the Lime Kiln as it was needed to mortar bricks at Bodie, Aurora and Del Monte. Later lime was also utilized in the cyanide process. Wood was stored at the Lime Kiln as it was used for fuel for the locomotives and the supply on the tenders had to be replenished at this point. The locomotive could haul 10 to 12 cars to the Lime Kiln; but since it was a heavy grade from there to Bodie, the train was broken up into sections. The locomotives then shuttled back and forth pulling 3 or 4 cars at a time into Bodie.

Newspaper item in 1881

The builders of the proposed Mono Railroad are Seth and Dan Cook, Robert W. Graves and H. M. Yerrington. It will be called the Bodie Railway and Lumber Co. The Bodie terminus will be on the ridge east of the old Bodie Works, the road passing the entire length of the mineral ridge, and after a zig zag descent and a series of loops, comes out on the eastern shore of Mono Lake on a 12,000 acre timber tract owned by the company. The road will be finished this summer in time for the fall wood business.

The dates and the newspaper item only hint at the history, romance, turbulent times and hard work connected with what the old timers referred to as "The Railroad in the Sky" and its counterpart, Mono Mills.

Locomotive near Bodie station in 1889.

Courtesy of McDonell sisters

Wood, lumber and cordwood were consumed at a prodigious rate by the booming town of Bodie, which was situated in a barren swale miles away from the nearest trees. Some wood was cut and brought in by burros and much of it was freighted up the steep slopes. J. S. Cain operated a steamer, S. S. Rocket (the ship had been hauled from Carson City by teams in 1879), on Mono Lake. Cordwood and lumber was cut and shipped across Mono Lake to Waford Springs where mule teams hauled it up to Bodie.

The railroad was built specifically to furnish the old mining town of Bodie with lumber and cord wood, both of which were important to keep the mines running and to supply the growing town. The Bodie and Benton Railway never served the town itself but only extended from the mining camp of Bodie to the timber at Mono Mills. It never was connected with an outside railroad although the possibility at times was it would be connected via Benton Station (7 miles were graded before the work was cancelled) with the Carson and Colorado Railroad. Surveys were also run across Mono Basin into Whiskey Flat and also Rattlesnake Canyon with terminals in Nevada. The little engines were not numbered but were given the colorful names of "Tybo", "Mono", "Inyo" and "Bodie". The "Tybo" was eventually worked at Keeler at the salt plant.

Superintendent Thomas Holt (an engineer) was in charge of construction and when the word was out that he needed men to put in

This sketch shows the Mono Mills platform and how they ingeniously utilized the drop of the ravine to slide their lumber down to the railroad tracks.

the railroad bed and rails, the notice attracted more Chinese than white men as the wages were low. So the Chinese were hired along with some white men. There was an excited meeting at the Miners Union Hall and a band of displeased men started the 21 mile hike to Mono Lake by foot, horse and buggy. Word preceded their approach and all the Chinese were put aboard the steamer Rocket and her scows (earlier purchased from J. S. Cain) and ferried out to Paoha Island. There the Chinese set up housekeeping with all their worldy goods. The frustrated miners arrived to find no one there, and no way to cross the water to the island. In their rush the miners had neglected

The sawmill was located in a draw with the upper story on the level with the surrounding area, so the logs were easily rolled into the mill. Circular saws were used here to cut the lumber but the planks were planed in Bodie.

— 52 —

These photographs were taken by Fred S. Brooks in 1904 when he worked at the Mono Mills logging camp, six miles out in the timber. Water tanker in background of top photo. The 16-mule team is pulling a 6-log

Mono Saw Mill later called Mono Mills was built 7 miles south of Mono Lake in 1881 as part of the Bodie Railway and Lumber Co. There were approximately 13,000 acres of pine timber at Mono Mills from which lumber and wood were cut. The sawmill supplied the mines of Bodie and Masonic, California as well as those of Aurora, Nevada.

to bring food and bedding and although some buggy loads of food and whiskey were sent to them, they soon dispiritedly straggled back to Bodie . . . where comments on the futile trip were not appreciated by the members of the excursion.

The train was never a passenger train, no fares were collected and passengers rode at their own risk.

The train started at Mono Mills 7 miles south of Mono Lake, proceeded to Warm Springs and then stopped at the Lime Kiln as some of the switchbacks were too steep for the engine to handle the entire length of cars. So the locomotive shuttled back and forth to haul all its cars up the grade.

"Michigan" buggies were used above Mono Mills to bring logs to the loading platform area in the woods. The West copied this unique manner of moving fallen trees through the forests from the Michigan logging camps. The wheels on the Michigan buggies were 10 foot high, and the immense logs were chained so the front end was held up and the back end of the log could drag. Earlier ten-oxen teams were used for pulling the logging trucks, some of which had solid wooden wheels. Teams of horses were used in later operations.

DAILY FREE PRESS.

VOL. III.   BODIE, CALIFORNIA, WEDNESDAY MORNING, OCTOBER 1. 1880.

THE DAILY FREE PRESS.   ASSAYING.   RESTAURANTS AND CHOP STANDS   OFFICE COLUMN
                                       Gold Hill Restaurant

PUBLISHED EVERY MORNING (EXCEPT
MONDAY) BY
OSBORNE & CLEVELAND.
RATES OF SUBSCRIPTION:

MISCELLANEOUS.
" Live and Let Live."

The Bodie Evening Miner.

No. 59.

BODIE, MONO COUNTY, CALIFORNIA FRIDAY, JANUARY 18, 1884   **GOLD!**   United States Bakery and Dining
                                                                        Rooms,
                                                                GEO. MILLER, Proprietor.

Society Meetings.

BODIE STANDARD.

VOL. I.   BODIE, MONO COUNTY, CAL., SATURDAY, JULY 6, 1878.   NO. 24.

The Tri-Weekly Standard

BODIE, SATURDAY, JULY 6, 1878.

THE FOURTH !

Complete Success of the Celebration.

Grand Procession in Our

Rivalry

Perhaps the newspaper rivalry started at the heighth of the boom in 1879, when a Truckee newspaper was quoted as saying that a little girl moving to Bodie ended her prayer, "Goodbye, God! We're going to Bodie."

The Bodie newspaper quickly responded that she was misquoted and that she had said, "Good, by god! We're going to Bodie."

NEVADA TRIBUNE, April 1878

Out in Bodie they have a preacher who "talks it so fine" that on one occasion, in speaking of the crucification of Christ he grew quite eloquent in describing the manner in which "they took the deceased down from the cross."

BODIE STANDARD, April 17, 1878

Hold on deacon! There is some mistake about this. If Bodie had ever been favored with the service of a preacher he might have used the language. But, fortunately, the spiritual interest of our people has been thus far utterly neglected.

1878

On December 9th, "Canty cut a man to pieces in Bodie, so private

advices state" . . . RENO RECORD. What we want to know is why can't a man get along in Bodie without fighting? — GOLD HILL NEWS.

BODIE STANDARD

Really, we can't say. It must be the altitude. There is some irresistible power in Bodie that impells us to cut and shoot each other to pieces. We feel ashamed to confess it, but we have frequently carved up eight or ten men while collecting items in the forenoon, without any reason which would seem a reason in a more solid atmosphere. All of the Standard corps are the same way. It is necessary to have an undertaking establishment in the building, and Mr. Friend has his rooms rent free for working off our private dead. The clashing of knives and the cracking of revolvers up and down Main Street can be constantly heard, and it sounds as though we were enjoying a perpetual Chinese Fourth of July. Scarcely a man in town wears a suit of clothes but has more or less holes in it, not as some would seek to make the credulous outside world believe, as a cause of the fall in stocks, and an inability to buy new ones, but because a man cannot go to his dinner without getting a bullet hole in his hat or the seat of his unmentionables cut away by the deadly knife of the desparado. Yes, it is sad, but only too true, that everybody must fight that comes to Bodie. However, Mr. "Canty" didn't cut anybody to pieces on the 9th of December, notwithstanding the private advices of the Reno Record. If the Record must know who cut that man to pieces—but we are not compelled to criminate ourselves. Bodie is indeed a hard place in the imagination of the imaginative.

November 1879

The following communication from Mr. H. Ward, the undertaker, gives the lie to the absurd stories going the rounds of the press about the ravages of pneumonia.

Editor Bodie Standard: Permit me, through your paper, to correct some misrepresentations which I read in the Virginia Enterprise of Sunday, headed, "A shocking condition of things in Bodie." In the first place there never has been twelve bodies, unburied, in Bodie at one time since I have been here—these last two years; the most at any one time was seven. The last month, October, there were 29 deaths. I buried all myself but one that was sent below for interment. The present month, November, up to the 17th, there have been twenty deaths all told. In regard to the County Supervisors refusing to bury the dead, that is also an error; but I have stated that the Board of Supervisors have passed my bills over from time to time since last April, and I had not received any renumeration for burying the dead since last April from that source; but I intend making some inquiry in respect to it. And I can further state, that at no time since I have been here has there been anything that would disgrace any community from an indecent burial, money or no money. The report about burying at night also is a fake in every particular.

H. Ward, Undertaker

1879

TOO TRUE

Over at Bodie the burial ground is so wet that they have to bail out the freshly dug graves to get the coffin in, and then they pile rocks on it to keep it from floating until the funeral is over, when the grave is filled with more rocks and with wet earth. At one place in the cemetery there is a coffin which is partly protruding from the ground, it having floated up from below. As the occupant was a Chinaman no notice can be taken of it. At the funeral services for these burials the preacher is at a loss to know whether to read the baptismal or the burial service.

THE DAILY FREE PRESS,
Monday, December 1, 1879

"The weather is so cold in Bodie that four pairs of blankets and three in a bed is not sufficient to promote warmth."—CARSON TRIBUNE

You are a brainless liar, and you can roll a cigarette, the weather here is delightful, in fact, it is too warm during the day for convenience as stiffs can not be kept any length of time without being packed in ice. And that article is very scarce and expensive. (The above was in a December paper).

June 1881

Bodie is becoming a quiet summer resort—no one killed here last week.

A Carson paper says that it looks as though half of the people of Bodie were Murderers. Carson should keep track of its brace faro games and let Bodie alone.

BISHOP CREEK TIMES,
Saturday, December 10, 1881

The BODIE FREE PRESS says there are two feet of snow on a level in that place. Here we have sunshine, dust and flies. Give us Bishop Creek or give us—money.

THE BODIE EVENING MINER,
April 8, 1884

Under column "Impromptu Outbursts" which were ads:

For a one horse paper, starting on a one horse basis, and doing business in a one horse way, by a one horse man, the progress of THE BODIE EVENING MINER has been wonderfully upward and onward.

TONOPAH BONANZA, 1909

It is now up to Bodie, if Bodie were blessed with a number of pretty little tots, that this city boasts of, we would not blame them to pull off a baby show. But as it happens the California town should not be jealous of the fact that the climate of Tonopah is considered the greatest in the West when it comes to raising kids.

The newspapers of Bodie: BODIE DAILY FREE PRESS, BODIE EVENING MINER, THE MINING INDEX, BODIE MINER — INDEX, BODIE STANDARD, DAILY BODIE STANDARD (merged with BODIE DAILY NEWS to form BODIE STANDARD-NEWS which eventually became the STANDARD NEWS), STANDARD NEWS (with various changes in title), BODIE WEEKLY NEWS, BODIE WEEKLY STANDARD-NEWS (also with variations in title).

Bodie Shops

Bodie Bank

August 1878

Fresh Fruit. Mr. G. Noble, of the Standard Market, keeps his stand constantly supplied with a large and varied assortment of fresh fruit, from Sonora and Sacramento, comprising apples, pears, bananas, apricots, strawberries, etc.

The spud famine has been relieved by the arrival in considerable quantities of that very useful vegetable.

A. Huntoon will deliver fresh and pure milk in and about Bodie at 50 cents per quart.

Two wagon loads of fruit, consisting of pears, apples and apricots from across the mountains, were on our streets Friday. The prices were not so very low.

The San Francisco Market on Main Street are receiving fresh fruits on every stage and have on hand: peaches, 20c per pound; plum, 35c per pound; pears, 25c per pound; oranges, 15 cents each; watermelon, o n e dollar each;

Interior of Burkham Merchantile Store in 1913. Standing left to right: Will Bell, Guy McGinnis, C. B. Burkham.

Courtesy of William Glenn

grapes, 25c per pound; eggs, 50c per dozen; cabbage, 10 cents each; cucumbers, 50c per dozen; green peppers, 25 to 50c each; summer squash, 20c per p o u n d; string beans, 15 to 25c per pound; fresh tomatoes, 15 to 25c per pound.

The Exchange Market of Aurora advertises that: beef by the side or quarter will be six cents per pound; mutton by the side, nine cents per pound; loin steaks, 16c per pound; coarser cuts 8 to 12c per pound.

April 1880

A wagon load of twenty pound trout came in this morning, and the fish found a ready sale at two bits a pound.

Daily arrivals of fresh strawberries at Kerschbraun, Son and Co., at 24c per box.

THE BODIE EVENING MINER
Thursday, March 13, 1884

J. F. Parker is up from Aurora with a load of spuds. They sell readily at five cents a pound.

When looking for fine fresh oysters, either on the half shell or cooked to order, or an especially choice breakfast be sure to patronize George Mann Jr.'s Laurel Palace Chop Stand.

Tuesday, March 24, 1884

By Stage—Received by stage today: Eggs and poultry to Boone; eggs to West; clams to Hirschberg; clothing to Wolf.

Tuesday, April 1, 1884
What Our Merchants Got By Stage.

Dry Goods and Notions for Jacobson. Ten cases of fresh eggs for C. H. West and Co. Clams for Louis Hirschberg. Printing material for the MINER. Cigars and tobacco for John Caldwell, Ed Gibson received a case of Eagle brand oysters, a large box of salmon, trout, flounders, and other fish. Siegel had a big case of fine cigars.

McKenzie Brewery which had an entrance to the right for the ladies. The McKenzie family inherited a sustaining feud with Mary McCann, the Irish janitress, when they purchased the brewery. Her house was on a lot adjoining the brewery and from there she waged her war of words, water and sometimes shots against the previous owner, Nick Carion.
Courtesy of McDonell sisters

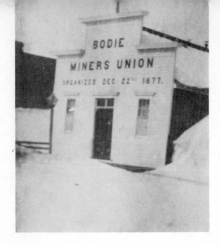

These are photographs taken and developed by Dr. Benjamin Franklin Surryhne who graduated with honors from the University of California Medical School in 1890. He went to Bodie to practice his profession in 1891 or 1892 and spent two years there. Top photo shows Bodie in the grips of winter. Center photo—Dr. Surryhne starting on medical rounds with satchel strapped to sled. Bottom left—Line-up in front of Wells Fargo Express—Figure on far right is Dr. Surryhne. Top left—Bodie Miners Union headquarters taken in 1891 or 1892. Dr. Surryhne was an active member of the Methodist church and sang in the choir while in his quarters was a piano ready for playing or for group singing.

Courtesy of Bancroft Library

Wednesday, April 16, 1884
The Union Market Still Ahead—Joe Hunt and Ben Potter delivered at the Union Market corral yesterday fifteen handraised, daisyfed, highly educated, muchly missed steers from the great ranges of Smith Valley. They're gentle, and they're kind; but strangers entering the corral are quickly tossed over the sixteen feet high fence. Eli Johl will spend Easter Sunday in dressing them for his army of customers, and Monday the Union Market will display as fine a lot of beef on the racks as can be produced anywhere or was ever seen in Bodie.

Friday, April 18, 1884
The stage today was partially loaded with poultry and vegetables for George Miller's fifty cents Sunday dinner. His twenty-five cents dinner are substantial and abundant, but of course the Spring chickens abhor that price and do not enter into the bill of fare in that department.

Tuesday, June 10, 1884
Those who are partial to bear meat can be supplied at the City Market, though Tommy Sara can't bear it.

Inyo Register
April 29, 1886
Bodie Items: FREE PRESS of the 23rd
Another cargo of eggs brought in yesterday by Flenniken, from Bishop Creek, another load of 600 dozen will get here by Sunday from the same region.

Lottie Johl standing in the doorway of the house Eli bought for her after finding her in the "Red Light District" and marrying her. This marriage almost broke up the flourishing butcher shop partnership of Donnelly and Johl as Mrs. Donnelly refused to accept Lottie. Annie Donnelly painted pictures and gave art lessons. Since the townspeople also ignored Lottie she had ample time to try to emulate Annie, and she too painted pictures. Some of these paintings are in the Bodie Museum. After the fire of 1932 this building was used as a post office with Mrs. Mary McDonell presiding as the last postmistress of Bodie.
Courtesy of McDonell sisters

Typical winter scenes of Bodie.
Courtesy of William Young
Courtesy of William Glenn
Courtesy of John Myers

NEWS EVENTS

September 1878

Jack O'Hara, who was mortally wounded Tuesday night, while attempting to jump a part of Black Hawk Mine, died Wednesday morning.

July 1879

The Explosion. Last evening, about dusk, a terrific concussion shook the entire district, instantly followed by a gigantic fountain of black smoke from the Standard hoisting works. The column of smoke shot into the air for a thousand of feet or more, and the top mushroomed into an umbrella in titanic proportions, soon spreading over the entire visible sky. The powder magazine of the Standard Works had exploded. Seven men were killed or later died from the injuries. Two were blown into atoms, no trace of them being recovered and scores were injured.

The funeral was the largest ever held in Bodie, 604 citizens being in line. All flags were at half mast and

The retort room at the foundry with the molten metal being made into bullion.

A. A. Forbes Photo

Courtesy of John Myers

Placering in Bodie.

Slum Pond at Standard Mine in 1913 with Dan McDonell standing and Harry Dolan by the ore car.

nearly every building was draped in solemn black and white bunting.

September 1879

This community was never more excited, never in greater danger of doing something or allowing something to be done, which would have left a dark stain upon its record, than on last Saturday. The tragic ending of the struggle between the Jupiter and Croyhee claimants for a small piece of mining ground—the killing of John Goff—created a deep feeling of resentment against the successful parties to the conflict, and their removal from town was probably the most sensible thing that could have been done. There was every indication during the day that had they remained there would have been bloodshed during the night. As it turned out the Miners Union and friends to the number of 500 or 600 armed men marched to the disputed property, forcibly demolishing and burning barriers. John Dinan, foreman of the Mono, who made some demonstration, was knocked down and cuffed about considerably.

The brunt of the resentment at the death of Goff fell upon George Daly, Superintendent of the Jupiter. The air was filled with threats Saturday that he would be killed that night and it was reported that a vigilance committee was forming to carry out the object.

Later, Daly was arrested and charged with murder. The officers

Hauling ore out of the tunnel. Bodie boasted of Old Tom, the educated mule who could count and tell time. Seems Tom could easily pull six cars of ore and would start out as soon as he heard the sixth click, but refused to move if there was a seventh click. Tom also quit working when he heard the noon and quitting time whistles.

A typical hoisting works.

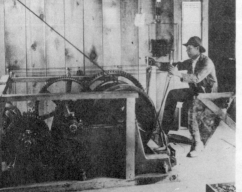

decided to remove Daly to Bridgeport at once, as a matter of pre-
caution and he was hurriedly taken
out of town under a strong escort
of Deputy Sheriffs. At Bridgeport
Mr. Daly must have given bonds,
as he proceeded to Carson.

It is, of course, very gratifying
that we have had no bloodshed. At
the same time, however, no thought-
ful man can contemplate the latter
with any great amount of satisfaction. A new power has arisen, entirely unknown to law, which as-
sumes to say who shall and shall
not live in Bodie. It appears that
within the limits of Bodie Mining
District, another qualification is re-
quisite. He may live here if the
Bodie Miners Union does not object
to him.

That being the case—as we would
like to stay here a while longer, if
no one objects — we make our
acknowledgements to the new power.

June 1880

THE GRAND BOUNCE
JUMPERS FENCE IN STANDARD AVENUE AND BUILD A HOUSE IN THE NIGHT. THE CITIZENS MAKE A RUSH AND WIPE THE "WHOLE WORKS" IN ONE MINUTE.

Courtesy of William Glenn
South End Cynide. Plont-Bodie (Late 1890).

January 7, 1884
GO IT BOYS—Some of the new-
ly made rich men of Bodie turned
loose last night. The thermometer
marked zero, but the boys fortified
with beef tea, coffin varnish and
Roderer, marched up and down
Main Street warming the midnight
air with the songs of all nations.
Some of the words were: "In the
mor-n-n-ing; in the bright light. I
could sing and never tire, Bodie
Mine, Bodie Mine." Through lack of
practice there was some discord, but
not enough to permanently cripple
the artistes. If we had Bodie stock
enough to improve our voices, we
would like to have joined them.

The Race Track located at Booker Flat.
Courtesy of Mervin McKenzie

Monday, January 14, 1884

THE McCLINTON HOISTING WORKS BURNED.

At a quarter past six o'clock this morning an alarm of fire was sounded. The cause proved to be the old McClinton hoisting works, which, of course was totally destroyed.

August 25, 1894

Standard Con. Hoisting Works burned about noon on Saturday last. The blacksmith shop at the Standard Hoisting Works at Bodie caught fire. When the alarm was given, Marshall's fruit team had just arrived from Sonora, and Mr. Marshall quickly unhitched his team and hitched his team to the fire engine and hauled it up the hill to the fire, but it was little or no use when it arrived there. The fire soon had caught the main building and it took but a short time to clear everything of combustible nature from the hill where the works had been, the scene of remunerative industry for nearly a score of years. A lot of lumber and about three hundred cords of wood went up in smoke, the latter we learn was not a company loss. It had not been accepted, the owners of it not having filled their contract. The works were of the best, nothing having been spared or overlooked in their erection to make them a credit to Mono county's old reliable. Consequently the loss is heavy, but fortunately no lives were lost, the miners getting out through the Bulwer works. The cage and cable dropped to the bottom of the shaft, the timbers of the shaft were charred about 20 feet. It was said that there was $30,000 insurance on the works, a sum that will be a great help to the company in rebuilding.

Dec. 1900

At one thirty o'clock this morning the hoisting works of the Goodshaw Mining Co. was entirely destroyed by fire. Four men were suffocated in the mine from the fumes of the fire penetrating into the shaft.

October 9, 1909

Fearful accident at Bodie. Nine men dropped 500 feet deep into the Tioga shaft.

Entertainment
Some Scheduled Some....

July 1878

Sheet and pillow slip party. B.S.S. Club will give a sheet and pillow slip party at Miners Union Hall on the evening of the eighth of August.

September 1878

The Bodie Silver Coronet Band will give a Grand Ball in Miners Union Hall on September 6 for the purpose of buying instruments.

September 1878

The SAN FRANCISCO VAUDEVILLE COMBINATION will appear in Bodie September 10th in drama, farces, songs, dances, Dutch specialties, banjo solos, etc.

October 1878

Snowshoe club. A movement is on foot to organize a snowshoe club for exercise during the coming winter.

Dec. 1878

The Bienvenu Club composed of fifty of the best young men of town, gave an invitational entertainment in Miners Union Hall, Saturday evening.

Bodie had many social and fraternal organizations and this photograph shows the enjoyment of those who celebrated this initiation night with a masquerade party.

Courtesy of John Myers

July 1879

A GRAND WALKING MATCH of 12 hours for $200 a side between Miss Viola Roseberry and Joe Kellog will take place at Miners Union Hall, July 18.

October 1879

The Council of the Bodie P.P.P. will on October 8th, give one of their unique balls at Miners Union Hall. Tickets admitting ladies and gentleman $3.

A LARGE CROWD OUT — LIVELY BETTING—FINE WEATHER—GOOD SPORT.

There was a large, though good humored — albeit, somewhat boisterous crowd out to see the races Sunday. The weather was splendid and the track in good condition. Pools were sold on the results at the Comstock saloon on Saturday night, and also on the ground just before the races came off. The first race was a quarter mile dash for $80. a side. The second, a quarter mile for $250. The third a quarter mile for a $200. purse, and the fourth was quarter mile heats, best two out of three, between two scrubs.

A special meeting of Bodie Commandery, Knights Templar, will be held at the Asylum Monday evening. All Sir Knights are requested to attend.

June, 1881

The faro banks are doing their share of the business; stud-horse poker draws moderate house, and keno is dull and normal. Dance houses are in demand with a liberal supply in the market.

The Bodie Jockey Club was organized on the 14th of the month, in the office of Judge Neuman.

Sadie Sturgeon (Mrs. Stuart Cain) and Jessie Murphy.

Courtesy of William Young

"Billy" Young tells: "During the winter of 1910-1911, Miss Cassin, a secretary to the Power Company, was on her way to the Occidental for dinner. The snow was so deep that you had to stoop down to get under the wires on Main Street. The snow had melted away from the buildings and sloped steeply toward the walls. Miss Cassin ducked under a line to get across, slid down the snow and slid directly into the dining room taking the window frame in with her."

McClinton Mine

Courtesy of McDonell sisters

Favorite spot for a picnic was "The Willows" back and above the racetrack.

The Metzger and Tom McDonald families have a portrait taken on the 4th of July, 1895.

Courtesy of Harry Metzger

4th of July

THE BODIE EVENING MINER,
Tuesday, January 22, 1884

Leap Year Party—The ladies will give their leap year party at Miners Union Hall on Friday evening. The Committee of Arrangements and the Floor Managers are offphay, and the party will be a nice one. Gentlemen must imagine they are not gentlemen—for one night only.

Thursday, January 24, 1884

A Rule—At the leap year party tomorrow evening, no gentleman, unattended will be permitted to cross the floor; but, should he desire to cross from one part of the hall to another, he will request the attendance of one of the floor committee, in the event of the absence of his escort.

Upper Grade, 1912. Bill Glenn wearing tall cap, second to the right of Harvey Eich, principal.

Courtesy of William Glenn

Wanted—Two partners for the Leap Year Party tomorrow evening, inquire at Mr. Stewart's drug store.

Gentlemen get even—Those young men, who, for the last four years have been compelled to patiently wait and hour and sixty minutes for their girls to primp their bangs, pencil their eyebrows, put on their kid gloves, etc, now have a chance to get even. Revenge is sweet, boys; so take advantage of this golden opportunity for it will be four long years ere you will have another such a chance.

THE BODIE EVENING MINER, Thursday, February 21, 1884

Three P Costumes—A mammoth truck full of most magnificent costumes for the masquerade ball tomorrow night got left over at Hawthorne. The truck will positively be received at Charley Kelly's tomorrow morning, when parties who have been relying on this shipment can call and select their costumes.

BODIE MINER, Feb. 13, 1909

News and notes of Bodie.—One week from Monday the big Masquerade Ball of the P. P. P.'s takes place and will be the event of the season. Be sure and be there if you desire to have a good time, leave your anti-dancing foot at home and join the merry throng in forgetting dull cares.

Get on your best bib and tucker, attend the Masquerade Ball next Monday night. The music will be good and the floor in fine condition. The crowds jolly and supper at the Occidental fit for a king. Everybody and his best girl and best boy will be there.

Bodieites recall with enthusiasm their childhood in Bodie. Several mentioned carrying lunches to "Papa" at the Standard Mill. Others remembered that the townspeople were so accustomed to the sound of the many stamp mills that if they stopped working, the silence would wake the soundest sleeper. Many Cornishmen (Cousin Jacks or Singing Jacks) were employed in the mines and the Cornish wrestling tournaments were an annual affair. By Chinese tradition, food was left on the graves after burial and these Bodieites tell you with amusement that not only did the Piute Indians eat this food, but that the children of the town enjoyed it too!

Courtesy of Mrs. Floris E. Harris

Sleigh dumped young couples out on the snowbank as they were on their way to a dance in Aurora. After dancing the night through at Aurora, it would be daylight when they returned to Bodie.

Harry Metzger was 9 years old in 1908 when his sisters and their husbands went on horseback trip to Yosemite Valley. Left to right: F. T. Roach, Mabel Metzger Roach, Harlan Burkham, Maud Metzger Burkham.

In the background—The Standard Mill at Bodie. In the foreground—boy with straw hat, F. I. Green.

...Some unscheduled

**RENO WEEKLY GAZETTE,
September 25, 1879**
A costly barroom mirror was demolished in Bodie last week by a stray pistol shot, which missed the barkeeper but shattered the glass.

February 19, 1880
Four dance houses in Bodie. In Bodie the other night a stalwart miner slipped on the floor of a dance house, and broke his leg.

June 1880
A wildcat and a bull terrier dog make the fur fly for one hundred dollars a side at Upper Dance House tomorrow night.

June 1880
The mining superintendent dared a hurdy girl, out on a dance hall, to fight him a few evenings ago and got a black eye for his temerity.

January 1878
Talk! Backtalk! Liar! Knives! Cause, whiskey. Damage, slight. All in an uptown saloon.

June 1878
On account of the sale of a drove of untamed mustangs on main street yesterday, and the fun of seeing them rode for the first time, business in Bodie was almost at a standstill.

November 1878
It has become a habit among many of our bucolic neighbors to ride a fiery, untamed mustang furiously through our otherwise quiet streets at breakneck pace (only they don't break their own necks), and thus endanger the life and lives of such unwary pedestrains as may be as unfortunately in their route. This practice is reprehensible and should be stopped.

December 1878

It is customary among lovers of pistol practice to engage in the rather questionable sport in out of way places or ranges, but with us here, the recreation is carried on in our streets, mostly at night. But we decidedly object to this favorite means of amusement.

October 1879

A dog fight and a run away horse were the excitements on Main Street yesterday evening. Main Street has more saloons in a given length than any thoroughfare in the world.

THE DAILY FREE PRESS, November 6, 1879

A four horse team from Sonora broke up the monotony a little last evening by taking a go-as-you-please run down Main Street. As they were not very ambitious no damage was done.

THE WASTE DUMP

Ducks are very abundant on Mono Lake and the sports are doing the shoot act in fine style.

BODIE EVENING MINER, Friday, January 18, 1884

Works of Art—Have you seen those beautiful panels at the Post Office Saloon? One has bunches of white lilacs and the other panel has purple ones, and they are so naturally painted that you can almost smell their fragrance. Those panels are to be raffled soon; secure your tickets at once.

Monday, January 21, 1884

Bodie has a chicken cock that will be backed against anything that stands erect on two legs and wears feathers and spurs.

Same date:

There is a cat in this town that will fight any other man's cat, either catch as catch can, or New Orleans style, across a rope. Particulars of Sporting Editor of THE MINER.

Thursday, February 21, 1884

Assessor Mc Alpin sleigh rode a dozen mites of girls and boys into estatic bliss this afternoon.

Saturday, March 15, 1884

This week some sport was had in Joe Rowse's back parlor between two well known businessmen of Bodie. An Irishman thought, $20 worth, that he could throw a certain French gentleman twice out of three times, catch as catch can. And he thought right.

"In and Out of Town" July 13, 1881

The wrestling during the week has absorbed much interest. Honorably conducted it is a manly and an exciting sport; but — Little boys should not fight or rassle. But they should read and write a whole passel.

THE BODIE MINER, Sat., Sept. 11, 1909

BODIE BUNCH WIN PRIZE AT LUCKY BOY

The Bodie boys had the pull! Last Monday morning the tug-of-war team left for the bonanza camp and came back with the long end

The great fire of June 23, 1932 was said to have begun in a house in the rear of the Old Sawdust Corner Saloon. This photo shows additions placed for movie set.
Courtesy of California Historical Society

A. A. Forbes Photo

Courtesy of Los Angeles County Museum

Courtesy of Mervin McKenzie

Courtesy of John Myers

of the rope and the prize of $100. Of course there wasn't a resident of Bodie who didn't feel positive that the boys would carry off all that was in sight in the way of prizes, but they believed in shouting the loudest after the victory was won.

The team, consisting of (see last week's Miner) did the business in 16 minutes and that settled the proposition to the satisfaction of all concerned. The Lucky Boys were good pullers, but it takes stayers to get away with the Bodie bunch.

On the 6th of July our town boys proved that they could win out against the nine from the camp of crooked streets and on their own ground Bodie tug-of-war team put it all over them. We of the town of high altitude are still game and are open to engagements in most any line.

Tuesday, June 24, 1884

Healthy Exercise—The Bowling Alley at the Sazerac is crowded nightly with those who like to roll ten pins and with spectators. George Majeau has a fine stock of refreshments and makes everything pleasant for the boys. Next door to the Laurel Palace Chop Stand.

Saturday, June 28, 1884

Cooled by Spray—This is the way the Temple Saloon keeps the celebrated Felsen beer so frigid and nice. It is a novelty to see the spray works in active operation. Call in and see for yourself.

The Bodie gymnasium is now the most popular resort in town.

May 1881

Mrs. Sandy Bowers, the famous Washoe seeress arrived in Bodie on Friday morning May 7th. Today she will be ready to receive her old Washoe friends in regards to the past, present and future, etc.

These succinct lines told the initiated the story of Eilley Orrum who married Sandy Bowers and how they became millionaires from the Comstock lode, Virginia City, then the vein of silver pinched out. Sandy Bowers died young and Eilley became a fortune teller to make a living. (Bowers Mansion is open to the public).

A. A. Forbes titled it "A Bodie Residence" and Bodietes remember it as the home of Nels Winters who earned his living cutting wood for others, although he gathered sagebrush for his own use. When walking across the flat he looked like a huge walking sagebrush, then piling it on top of his building, he then used the sagebrush as fuel during the winter.

Courtesy of Los Angeles County Museum
A. A. Forbes Photo

The 4th. of July

Flags were hung; red, white and blue bunting was draped on the buildings; cottonwoods were hauled into town and placed in buckets along Main Street; everyone dressed in their Sunday best—and the mood was set for the year's biggest event in Bodie—Independence Day.

The drilling contests were usually held on Labor Day as were the mucking contests.

There were spirited baseball games between the mining camps.

Courtesy of Cecil Burkham

Bodie celebrated many occasions but Bodieites remember with nostalgia and fond memories the 4th of July celebrations. Bunting was placed on the false fronts of the buildings; cottonwoods were cut and brought into town and nailed to the uprights of the porches and placed in cans alongside the street; folks wore their Sunday best; drilling contests, three legged races and other contests were held so everyone could participate; floats were prepared and the organizd groups gathered in their regalia to march in the parade.

The July 6, 1878 newspaper's banner headlines:

THE FOURTH
COMPLETE SUCCESS OF THE CELEBRATION
GRAND PROCESSION IN OUR STREETS
THE LITERARY EXERCISES AT THE HALL
THE BARBECUE
A MATCH GAME OF BASEBALL
FUNNY FEATURES OF THE FESTIVE CREW
THE WAR DANCE OF THE PIUTE INDIANS
THE DAY CLOSED WITH THE MINERS'
UNION BALL

The three-legged race was as enthusiastically watched as it was run by the participants. The Fourth of July was a festive time—games to play, floats to prepare and to ride in the parade, marching either with the bands or with your fraternal group, baseball games, dining out at one of the hotels and then the finale, the Grand Ball.

THE FESTIVE CREW
(Popularly termed "The Horribles").

About three o'clock the merry makers could be seen slipping out of back doors in different parts of town and repairing to the rendezvous near the Miners Union Hall. They soon started out on their predatory march, and a grotesque looking crew they certainly were. At their head, mounted on a crazy mustang, came their leader, Gen. Blucher, whose office was that of grand Bombshell. His horse "Bobbed" him up and down a good deal, but he "Gurled" his legs under pretty well and hung on.

Following Gen. Blucher came the Band, blowing tin horns, ringing bells, playing triangles and beating gongs, and making a most discordant noise, led by a huge Drum Major.

After the Band came the "Horribles," some in wagon, some on foot, but a majority were mounted on donkeys. The disguises were so complete that very few of the crew knew each other. One wagon was made to represent a mounted cannon, a huge piece of pipe for an engine answering for the gun. It was drawn by a spiked team, and as the occupants of the wagon were constantly firing off bombs, making a terrific noise, the horses were nearly frantic . . .

Among the motley throng was noticeable his satanic majesty in a suit of red, with a prodigious long long tail. As usual he was up to all sorts of mischief, and as the principal objects of his ill will, Coxcombs came to grief all along the line of march. Humpty-Dumpty was well carried out by the butcher boy. Henry the Fifth wobbled around with a game leg; cause, too much gymnastics. The Knight who read the Declination of Indifference was sick the next day and should have taken some of his own prescriptions. The Esquimaux was also out in full force. The Spanish Knight, but for his armor, would have been taken for a Welch man. Francis the First found time during the parade to hop over the back of several Don Keys. German father did first rate, and his replies to the orator of the day were very good. That Dutchman was a holy terror. That big Figaro could have been Senter-ed by a good shot 200 yards. After marching up and down the streets, two, or three times, and creating no end of fun, they brought up at Miners Union Hall, from the steps of which the literary exercises, consisting of a "Horrible Poem," a Declination of Intentions and an Oration, more horrible than the poem, took place.

A. A. Forbes Photo
Courtesy of Nevada Historical Society

Note original Standard on the left while in this view the M. E. Church (original minister, Rev. F. M. Warrington) and the Catholic Church (original pastor, Father John B. Cassin) are in line with each other.

The Fourth of July was celebrated with much pomp and ceremony and patriotism ran high. A clipping from the 1880 newspaper:

One large flag attracted particular attention. It was flying from a staff set on the highest point of Bodie Bluff. The Committee had determined that the flag, should be there but as they had neither staff nor flag, for the moment were nonplussed. They finally picked up the staff, a piece here, a piece there, spliced them together and a good staff was the result. The material for the flag was acquired in a similar manner. The work started Sunday noon and at 4 p.m. the flag was flying. The committee are entitled to the unbounded thanks of the community.

The Methodist Church is on the far left while DeRoche's two story brick house which later became the County Hospital is center front of photo. The large white structure behind the Hospital is the United States Hotel. The original school house can be seen two blocks from downtown with the original Standard in the background. When this schoolhouse burned down, the Bon Ton Lodging House was moved to a new site to serve as a school. Both of these photographs on this page are unusual in that they show painted buildings.

Christmas

The McDonell sisters of Reno, who spent their childhood in Bodie, recall the fun of Christmas. Two Christmas trees were brought in and set up in Miners Union Hall. There were committees to assure that the evening would be a grand affair. Every family brought their gifts and these were checked in before they were placed under the Christmas trees. In the days when candles were used to light the Christmas trees, guards stood by with wet sponges on long sticks to douse any incipient flame.

FROM THE SAN FRANCISCO CALL of December 25, 1898

On December 24, 1880, I was up in Bodie with Dan Callarner a prospector. We were anxious to reach the mining property of the Homer Co., and though it was 28 miles from town and a blinding snow storm had set in, we started early, hoping to get there before nightfall. We had gone only a short distance when we began to regret starting on such a trip on such a day, but we determined not to turn back, although the snow was falling so thickly that we had to trust almost entirely on the horses to keep the rough road. About 10 miles from town, however, we were very nearly thrown out of the sleigh by a sudden jump of our animals to one side, which landed the outfit on a heavy drift. We found the cause to be a man lying apparently dead in the snow. After resuscitating him, he told us that he had started for Lundy, and had become exhausted and had given up in despair. He was poorly clad and very dejected, saying he had no friends and that he would be better off dead, but we took him into the sleigh, intending to give him a lift to his destination which we were to pass thru.

Courtesy of John Myers

The added weight made things worse for our horses, and by 9 o'clock at night we had only reached the house of George Barnes at the junction of the main road and the Mill Road, where we obtained permission to remain until morning. George and his little girl had retired but Mrs. Barnes was up dressing a Christmas tree, and she gave us a good hot supper and a bed and lent the old man blankets enough to make him comfortable in the barn on the hay.

The next morning we rose early, as the little girl roused the house with her joy over her presents, and I went out to see the horses. I found the old man much refreshed by his sleep and brought him in with me to breakfast. The child took a fancy to him at once and show- ed him her toys. A book had her name "Jessie Barnes" written on a leaf, and the old man eagerly asked her father's name. George came in just then and the stranger stood up and held out his hand.

"Don't you know me?" he said. "If you are the son of Jessie and Richard Barnes, you ought not to have quite forgotten my face."

And George put his arms around the old man's neck and said, "Father!"

It was a long story about their separation—Richard had come to California while his son was a mere boy, hoping to mend his fortunes, but things had gone wrong and he had lost track of his family.

Reaching manhood, George had come out here also, but he had prospered and had a comfortable home in which to care for his father in his old age, now that strange combination of circumstances had brought the two, who had not seen each other for over twenty years, together again.

"Santa Claus brought me lots of presents and a grandfather, too," said little Jessie. *"I think he is better to me than he is most little girls."* *... And I think he was.*

Xmas Story—Calif. Historical Society

Courtesy of California Historical Society

Courtesy of William Glenn

The winter of 1878-1879 was a most severe one. Wind, snow and blizzards whipped the flimsy wood frame houses. Since the town had been a small one, the rush of newcomers overcrowded the accommodations with the result that there was not enough housing, not enough wood, not enough food and not enough employment. Many deaths resulted from disease and exposure. The idle spent their time gambling, drinking and fighting with the resultant deaths.

Courtesy of California Division of Beaches and Parks

Indians

Feb. 1878

A drunken Piute Indian seeks some sunny, secluded spot, and rolls up in his blankets and mutters: "Piute, he heap big fool," and falls calmly, peacefully and soundly to sleep. The intoxicated white man howls and hoots himself home, smashes the furniture and the heads of any of the family who had not been warned in time to leave town, and altogether acts first class degenerate.

June 1878

Captain Bob, Chief of the Piutes in this neighborhood, has recently been made happy by the event of a son and heir. Now the owner and superintendent of the Red Cloud, at which the Captain receives "heap hogadie," the papoose has been named "Colonel Blasdel," by his proud father.

June 1878

Captain George, chief of the Piutes, came into town Sunday evening with 12 or 15 braves at his heels, and marching up to Mr. Wolf, one of the 4th of July finance committee, requested a sack of flour, and told him that they had come over from Walker River to dance a Sioux war dance on the 4th. The flour was given him.

July 6, 1878

Wednesday morning someone told the Piutes that the Carson Band which arrived on the stage, was the advance guard of a large party of soldiers who were coming here to kill them, and inside of an hour not an Indian was to be seen. They had fled to the mountains and sent a deputation to town asking "What

for you heap kill Piute?"

The matter was soon explained to them and that evening and the next day they all came back.

About 6 P.M. the bucks formed in line on the hill north of town and came down chanting a low guttural wail and moving sideways. Some of them had painted their faces entirely black and then besmeared them with streaks of white paint. It was a horrible sight. Every now and then the chiefs would run ahead of the band in a stooping position, jump from side to side and wail, and draw their bows as though an enemy had been sighted; then creep along further, run up and down the line, and acted almost like lunatics. This was heartily enjoyed by the onlookers, though it was evident that many of the Indians were adepts and no doubt have danced the "War Dance" under other and less favorable circumstances for their pale faced brethren.

October 1878

Pine Nut Season. Now is the time that ye gentle savage hies himself to the mountains and suns himself, while his faithful, although much abused, squaws engage plucking the fruit so dear to the Indian palate, and which we call pine nuts. Until the food is all gathered we shall miss the cheerful presence of the painted warrior and the dusky, dark-eyed maiden from our midst; but they will return to annoy many a good housekeeper with broken promises made of bringing water and cutting wood for family uses.

December 1879

Pogonip—beware! At sunrise this morning the air was filled with myriads of crystal frost which glittering in the bright sunlight, gave the atmosphere the appearance of being filled with diamond dust. This is the notorious "Pogonip," so termed by the Piutes, and according to them is the cause of all sickness.

When this condition of the weather occurs, all the Indians stay close to the wickiup, with a fire handy to heat the air with which to repel the danger of these minute particles of ice, which are floating about in the ether.

Friday, March 14, 1884

We saw Jimmy Warren's two little girls packing their dolls Piute style yesterday. They had two nice hobees just the right size to strap their play babies into, which were suspended from their foreheads in true Indian fashion.

As one oldtimer tells it, there was one Indian buck that always responded to your questions with "Guess so" . . . and soon he became known as "Guesso."

Harry Metzger tells that Guesso's wife did the washing for his mother and it was the custom that not only did the squaw come to do the wash and have her lunch with the family she was working for . . . but also her family came along. One day when they were having lunch Guesso was along as usual and spied the bar of soap nearby and picked it up and took a healthy bite!

A. A. Forbes, the photographer entitled this picture "Guesso's Camp." The Piute Indians built crude shelters of boards, rags, sagebrush on the hills surrounding town. In the evening their dwellings and the people were silhouetted by the bonfires and the smell of burning sage would drift down into town.

A. A. Forbes Photo   Courtesy of Los Angeles County Museum

Chinese

November 1879

Rout the Fiends. Tuesday night Constable Kirgan got in front of one of the opium dens in Chinatown, and blew his police whistle. Such a stampede as ensued has not been witnessed since the Blandensburgh Races. A series of clothes lines were encountered in the rush, and some of the prettiest ground and lofty tumbling ever seen was unveiled right there in the darkness. Kirgan contented himself with letting the "fiends" break their necks getting away, and some of them will remember these clothes lines for some time to come.

December 1879

The funeral procession of the Chinese woman who committed suicide, passed up Main Street this afternoon, and attracted a good deal of attention, and—strange as the assertion may appear—elicited considerable merriment. The coffin was in a sleigh containing the undertakers assistants and two other Chinese women. Next came Al Morgan, of the Old Tuolumne Stables, driving a beautiful little cutter with a bareheaded Chinese woman sitting by his side—the crowds on the sidewalks jeering Al in a good natured manner. Next came a short cutter with a long wagon bed on top, and in the wagon bed were seated about a dozen Chinese women, weeping and wailing as though their hearts were breaking into small fragments. But every time the little short cutter would "flop" over a ridge in the snow, the long wagon bed leaped into the air, standing first on one end and then on the other, each leap being punctuated by a cessation of the artificial wailing, and a sudden chorus of genuine feminine squeals and cries of alarm, and a wild scramble for a hand hold on the side of the wagon bed. Then, just as suddenly, an even keel would be resumed and without cracking a smile the terrible wailing and weeping for the dead would again break forth. Behind this followed three or four other vehicles filled with Chinese. It was most heart rendering to observe the painful attempts of the driver of the little short cutter with the long wagon bed superimposed, to maintain a look of solemnity as the dozen female mourners poured their wails into his ears as his little cutter reared up and down over the bumps in the snow like a whithall boat in a choppy sea.

February 1880

The noisy festive deeds of the Chinese New Year are upon us. The last three days Chinatown has been a perfect pandamonium of noises made up by gongs, drums, bombs and firecrackers.

June 1881

Another invoice of Chinamen arrived Monday to work on the railroad.

July 1881

A pleasant prospect. Sam Chung sat in an armchair on the verandah at his house in Chinatown, smoking a large meerschaum pipe; lolling in front of an opium den were three or four celestials pleasantly chatting about nobody knows what; a small dirty, but healthy child sat playing with an Indian dog and an old Mexican watched the twain with a pleased expression upon his face; a game of "pan" was in progress in several dens and the voices of merry makers could be plainly heard; the soft strains of a Chinese guitar mingled with the general humdrum, and t h e signboards creaked on their hangings and the mild breezes floated past. This was the scene that presented itself on King Street at 3 o'clock yesterday afternoon.

January 26, 1884

Chinese New Year—Tomorrow at midnight the annual infliction of Chinese New Year will begin, and for eight consecutive days and nights a suffering public will be treated to an explosion of bombs, the pop of firecrackers, the hubbub of the gong, and screech of the Chinese fiddle. We should be thankful, at least, that Chinese New Year, like the American variety, comes but once a year.

May 2, 1884

A Chinaman will be tried at one o'clock Monday for having Doc. Roger's game cock in his possession without having the Doctor's permission.

Tuesday, May 6, 1884. The Chinamen who stole Dr. Roger's hens were fined $30 and $21 respectively. They found it very expensive chicken.

Dr. B. F. Surryhne's photo of a busy street scene was taken in 1891 or 1892 and shows the diversified types of people who came to a mining camp.

Courtesy of Bancroft Library

These scales were used to weigh both opium in the opium dens and also the gold dust on the bars of the saloons in Bodie.

Power by Wire

GREEN CREEK

Bodie made history in December 1, 1892 by completing construction of a hydro-electric power plant at Green Creek and then transmitting the electrical power overland for industrial purposes to the Standard Mill. Tom Legett, Superintendent of the Standard Consolidated Mining Company, persuaded the reluctant stockholders that power transmission was possible, for up to this time electricity had only been used at its source. However, the engineers were given instructions to build a line without curves or angles as it was believed the power would jump off if the line was not straight. So the venture known as "Legett's Folly" was a success and the word spread over the world creating a scramble for power sites. Power was not delivered until October 1893 due to delays and accidents. The editor of the CHRONICLE UNION of Bridgeport visited Green Creek and tells of his experiences in the June 10, 1893 issue.

The Standard Con. Electric Plant. On Monday, in company of Postmaster Bryant and family, we visited the Standard Con. Electric Power House on Green Creek, 8 miles south of Bridgeport, over an excellent route, the portion of the Dunderberg Road having been built by the Standard Con.

At the plant we found manager T. H. Legett and family, the latter having come over on their way to Bridgeport to spend a few days, and all were hospitably received although visitors are not desired just yet, but when the works are in perfect running order, due notice will be given when visitors will be welcome.

The power house is 30 x 40 feet, substantially built with a very steep roof, so that no snow will stay on it long. Green Creek furnishes water power through a ditch, the lower end of which is 355 feet above the power house, giving a pressure of over 150 pounds to the square inch. The pipe from the penstock leads into a steel receiver, 40 inches in diameter and 9 feet 8 inches long, from which four tapered pipes lead the water under pressure of 350 feet vertical head onto four 21-inch pelton water wheels, each pipe being fitted with two nozzles, the water from one striking the wheel on the lower right hand side and the other underneath left hand side, each wheel developing 62½ horsepower, or 250 for the four. These wheels run at 365 revolutions, although while working in our presence it got away with 920 revolutions. The wheel shaft is connected by a patent insulating coupling to the armature shaft of a Westinghouse, 120 kilowatt alternating dynamo, generating current at 3,500 volts. A Doolittle governor is attached to the wheels, and a number two pelton wheel runs the "exciter," required for generating the initial current fields of the large machine.

The pole line from the dynamo to the motor of the company's mill at Bodie is about 12½ miles, the poles are large and substantial put up to withstand the heaviest winter storms, the poles are being put 100 feet apart. The current delivered at the mill will be of 3000 volts tension. The Mill and Power House are connected by telephone.

The Motor Room at the Standard Con. Mill at Bodie is 26 x 18 feet. The motor is 120 horsepower, and will be brought up to speed by a small motor of 3 to 4 horsepower which is built on the same bed plate with the larger and, thrown out of circuit when the latter is running at the proper speed. At the works in Bodie there will be two transformers of 100 incandescent lights capacity each for lighting the mill and company's office. The plant has cost about $30,000, which the company will soon get back in the reduced cost of running its mill, etc. As there will be a saving of nearly $1,500 a month in the matter of wood alone.

The work of putting the plant in running order is in the hands of H. M. Reid (Reed?), Chief Electrician, who recently came out from Pittsburgh, who is also President of Standard Con. When the plant is in successful running order, it will be accepted by Mr. Legett, and the works at Bodie will be started up again.

Works were set up in motion during our visit, and everything seemed to be working nicely. As soon as the plant at the power house is satisfactorily in running order, Mr. Reid will go to Bodie and put the motor in order, and make connection with the power house. The successful inauguration of this enterprise will revolutionize mining and milling in this county, and many companies with ores will utilize them.

While the Standard Con. made history with their transmission of power from Green Creek to their holdings in Bodie in 1892, it was not until 1910 that the Hydro Electro Company at Jordan provided lights and power for the town of Bodie.

HYDRO ELECTRO COMPANY AT JORDAN
April 28, 1910, BODIE MINER

Actual construction work commences. Supplies for power plant in route from Minden to Jordan. Some ideas of the

The Standard Mill interior as it looks today showing a portion of the 20-stamps.

size of the plant can be had by the construction calls for 12,000 feet of wooden pipe, 48 inches in diameter and 3100 foot of steel pipe from 48 inches down to 36 inches. The plant will be in operation by the first of August. The freight coming along for the hydro-electric plant at Jordan is in at Thorn—two transformers weighing 12 ton each. This will make it necessary to build a steel track for carrying. The dynamos are monsters being 12 foot high and 11 feet wide. Which will manufacture juice to burn.

December 24, 1910, BRIDGEPORT CHRONICLE-UNION

Juice will arrive in Bodie on Christmas.

The Hydro Electro Company is stringing wires for the distribution of light and power to the residents of Bodie. The pipeline is completed and it is expected that the juice will be turned on Christmas Day.

Courtesy of California Division of Beaches and Parks

Buildings at Mill Creek plant prior to slide of 1911.

Hauling the generator to Mill Creek.

Courtesy of William Glenn

Buildings at Mill Creek plant prior to slide of 1911.

Interior of the Mill Creek Plant prior to the avalanche of 1911.

After the avalanche.

Avalanche

AVALANCHES BRING DISASTER, DESTRUCTION AND DEATH
Nine Lives Lost Relief Parties Are Searching For Bodies of Unfortunate Victims.

BUILDINGS OF PACIFIC POWER COMPANY AT COPPER MOUNTAIN ARE DEMOLISHED
Electric Plant at Crystal Lake Gold Mining Company at Lundy is Buried Under a Mountain of Snow.

Like a thief in the night, the mountainside came to the valley, took the lives of those in its path, leaving broken hearts and desolate homes in its wake. As soon as the news of the calamity was known willing hands took up the work of rescuing those who perchance might be alive or the bodies of those beyond human aid. The mines of Bodie are closed and an army of shovelers are opening a road to Copper Mountain, 20 miles distant. Meantime the rescue work at the power plant is progressing rapidly.

RESCUED ALIVE
Mrs. R. H. Mason. Yesterday the rescue party found Mrs. Mason alive and she was taken to J. A. Conway's, where every

care and attention is being given her. With her husband she occupied one of the cottages that was destroyed and for nearly 60 hours was entombed in the wreckage. Reports this morning indicate that she will recover.

BODIES RECOVERED

R. H. Mason
John Sullivan
a miner, who was occupying a cabin a short distance from the power plant.

The Rescue Party is Making Good Progress and Expect to Find the Other Bodies Today.

The storm this week has been the most destructive to life and property of any in history of the county—so far nine lives being lost in snow slides.

About 2 o'clock Wednesday morning the power and light went off at Bodie and investigation proved that a snowslide had demolished the building of the Pacific Power Company at Jordan and that eight lives were lost in the disaster. Those dead are: R. H. Mason, H. M. Weir, E. M. Peacock, Harold Hardy, Ben Pessner, John Sullivan, Patrick Stromblad. As soon as the news of the terrible accident reached Bodie Thursday forenoon relief parties were organized and in a few hours nine men on snowshoes started for Copper Mountain. Later in the day another party left for the scene of the disaster in an effort to relieve the situation. Linemen, Paul Green-

Mrs. Mason's cottage at Mill Creek after snow slide.
Courtesy of California Division of Beaches and Parks

leaf, of the Pacific Power Co. and L. A. Larson of Bodie were the first to learn of the catastrophe. Wednesday morning they left Bodie to locate what was supposed to be a break in the line and traveled the entire distance to the power plant, which was found wrecked and covered with slide.

They went to Mono Lake in an endeavor to communicate with headquarters, but found the telephones at Mattley's and Hammond's out of commission. Going to C. W. Bogt's place they finally reached the Bodie office by the way of Mono Mills Thursday morning.

The scene of the accident is 20 miles from Bodie where a power plant of 2000 horsepower was installed last year by the Hydro Electric Company and turned over to the Pacific Power Company at the first of the year. The pipeline from Lundy, a distance of 7 miles, carries the waters of Mill Creek along the north side of the canyon and around to the east side of Copper Mountain, where there is a fall of 1500 feet to the power house.

The building was a one story concrete structure and the machinery therein was the most modern. Two concrete cottages were built to accommodate the employees and the slide demolished these as well as the power house.

Under ordinary conditions the buildings would be considered safely situated as they stood nearly 1000 feet from the steep part of the mountain, but the unusually heavy snow upset all calculations and the catastrophe arrived.

While the buildings were wrecked, the machinery was but slightly damaged. At one time a smelter was in operation there in a building that has stood there since 1879, was destroyed by the big slide, as were sereval other structures nearby that had been erected 30 years.

The lines were furnishing power and light to Bodie, Lucky Boy and Hawthorne and would be supplying the mines and mills of Wonder, Nevada. It is believed that the plant will be in operation again soon.

Saturday March 18, 1911
Clearing up wreck of the disaster. The terrible snowslides of last week that destroyed the life and property at Jordan, Lundy and Masonic are the worst ever known in the county. The power plant at Jordan, where the greatest loss of life took place, was only erected last summer and the current was turned on last Christmas Day furnishing light and power for Bodie, California, Aurora, Lucky Boy, Hawthorne, Fairview and Wonder, Nevada.

Con Pacific Mine

Andrew Sturgeon and Ted Corrington, two members of the rescue team that traveled to Jordan.

After Mrs. Mason was dug out from her 60 hour entombment in the snow, the rescue team took her to the Conway Ranch, then to Bodie from where she went to San Francisco for medical attention.

Church

December 1878

We have no church, but Miners Union Hall answers that and a variety of other purposes. On Saturday evening, for instance, the hall was occupied for a "grand testimonial a n d complimentary benefit to Billy Costello, the champion lightweight of the Pacific Coast," matched to fight Harry Maynard for $1000, a side. The performance closed with a rattling "passage at arms" between Billy Costello and Cassidy. At ten o'clock Sunday morning the Rev. Father Cassin, of the Roman Catholic Church, said mass in the same place, but dismissed his congregation in time to allow Rev. G. B. Hinkle, of the Methodist Episcopal Church, to preach to his little flock, at 2 p.m. In the evening the platform of the same hall was occupied by an amateur minstrel performance, on which occasion were not a few of the dead and buried jokes of the past generation perpetrated upon the present one.

March 1879

Bodie in boasted progress and improvement has evidently forgotton what she needs most — that is a church; a big one with a spire as high as our expectation and spring developments. It ought to make the very boulders blush when the fact is made known that Mono County never had, not even the semblance of a church building. Our neighbor, Inyo County, is not much better off in grace for they have but one building of the kind, one erected by a little band of laborers in Bishop Creek. It stands there as a noble example, and it used to do our souls good to witness the peculiar manner in which the young pumpkin raisers done their sparking while the old folks exhorted.

October 1879

Bodie is probably the only city of 8000 inhabitants in the world which has no church. It is also the only place at which Pinafore was never sung until last night.

December 1879

Divine Services. Divine Services tomorrow at Odd Fellow's Hall at 11 A.M. and 7 P.M., G. B. Hinkle officiating. All are cordially invited to attend.

Reverend Hinckle Society entertains. A church sociable will be given by the ladies of Reverend Hinckle Society tomorrow evening. The best of music and a choice dramatic entertainment is down on the programe.

Oysters, lemonade, candies, fruits and popcorn balls for refreshments. A pleasant time together with a profitable social gathering is anticipated. Let everybody attend.

April 1880

Rev. Mr. Hinkle will soon commence the erection of a Methodist Church on Green Street, above Fuller — an excellent location.

WEEKLY STANDARD NEWS and FREE PRESS,
June 8, 1881
Bodie to have church. Subscription started at that time for the use of Rev. F. M. Warrington of the M. E. Church.
BODIE EVENING MINER, Saturday, June 14, 1884
Methodist Episcopal Church—T. P. Bradshaw, Pastor, Sabath Services: 10:30 a.m., Sunday School 7:30 p.m., song, service and preaching. Prayer meeting every Thursday at 7:30. *Seats free.* You will be cordially welcomed.
St. John's Catholic Church—Father James Melvin, Mass every Sunday morning at half past ten o'clock. Sunday School at 1:30 p.m. Vespers in the evenings at 7:30. *Seats free,* and all are cordially invited.

1883

Methodists finally built a church building on Green Street, but, it is supposed that, as the saloon and gambling element was very much depleted, the funds were secured by popular subscription and not from a tax on these establishments, as one of our facetious newspaper correspondents suggested. The Catholics also constructed a church, St. John the Baptist, on Wood Street.

Team owned by A. G. Allen, West Point Ranch, Mono Lake, Calif.
Jerk line team entering Bodie in 1911. In the background is the Catholic church, St. John the Baptist. Just to the right and out of the picture would be the McKenzie Brewery.
Courtesy Nevada State Museum

Following is a letter written to a mother who had inquired of the minister about her son.

Bodie, Cal.
Jan. 25/81.

Mrs. Thomas D. Penfield
  Dear Madam:

Your communication of 10" ult. came duly to hand. I purposed being more prompt with a reply, but the multiplied duties of a minister in such a field as this have caused the delay.

You will know that I was not greatly surprised at your addressing me when I state that your letter is not the only one of the kind I have received from an anxious mother. Only yesterday I answered one to which my reply was not, and could not be, so welcome as this. The party inquired for was what, in the phraseology of this coast, is termed a "hoodlum", in plain Anglo Saxon a ruffian. I have a better report of your son, not that I can give a full account of him, for I have not had opportunity to learn; but he has been present at some of my services, and says he comes when he can. His address is that of a gentleman, and I understand he gives his employers satisfaction by faithful service. From his reception of me and my assistant S. Sch. Supt., whom I introduced to him, I am disposed to think he is not averse to good influences. At the same time I do not wonder that you tremble when you think of his surroundings, "a sea of sin," lashed by the tempests of lust and passion. Such dissipation as is indulged in here you never have read of in books. No man can write it. Let me give you the table of contents for last week's chapter in Bodie: On Monday morning a man was lynched for shooting another in cold blood the week before. On Friday two men grappled each other, and holding fast with left hands poured shot into each other until one dropped dead, and the other has been expected to breathe his last each hour since.—Fill that out with what you must know accompanies it, and you have one week. But for your comfort I must say that no man is in such dangers, except by his own choosing. Respectable citizens feel as safe as in our well regulated cities, and I think your son is one of that number. Advise him to attend our Sunday School and preaching services. I will befriend him as I can.

Rspfly. Rev. F. M. Warrington.

Cemetery

Ten thousand people lived in the high barren swale and perhaps because of their isolation, the townspeople made an occasion of every
funeral and the two plumed hearses were much in demand. When
Bill Bodey's bones were found an impressive funeral was arranged for
the reinterment. When President Garfield died from his assassination
wounds, the citizens proceeded to drape the town in black and white
bunting, an elaborate casket was placed in the shiny hearse with the
plumes, the riderless horse was led with reversed boots in the stirrups
and all marched in stately procession to the cemetery on the hill. There
were unexpected incidents, too. A Chinese man hired the hearse for
the burial of his wife and had the band accompany the funeral group.
On the return trip down the hill the band played, "The Girl I Left
Behind Me"; the horses became frightened and bolted; and the entire
affair ended in confusion.

1882—35 years old
Amiable, she won all
Intelligent, she charmed all
Fervent, she loved all
And dying, she saddened all.

**DAILY FREE PRESS,
December 3, 1879**

KEEP THE GATE CLOSED! Someone left the gate of the cemetery open last night and let in a terrible draft of cold air. It was so cold, that Bill Bodey got up and shut the gate with such a slam that both hinges were broken off. The residents of that section state that his language, on the occasion, frightful.

Tuesday, December 9, 1879

An interesting case was on trial today in Peterson's court, in which Pat Brown, plaintiff and H. Ward, defendant. From the testimony it appears that Brown has dug 30 graves, and charged $162 for his services. 25 of these graves were occupied—the balance remaining tenantless. Brown claimed that all he received was $17. The question arose as to whether he should receive pay for the uninhabited graves he had dug. The jury returned a verdict for the plaintiff—$123.

**December 21, 1879
"A Grave Question"**

Pat Brown suing H. Ward, undertaker, for $146 due for services rendered digging graves. During the trial it came out that it cost more to bury a rich man than a poor man— comment causing merriment among the spectators. It was explained that a rich man's coffin was placed in a big box but a poor man was buried in a box just the size of the body. Jury returned verdict in favor of plantiff for the sum of $124.

Courtesy of William Glenn
Funeral of Jack Jeffries on January 19, 1913.

Belvidere Mine

Patrick Phelan, Bodie
Policeman.

Bodie jail.

Courtesy of California Division of Beaches and Parks

Bad Men or Bad Shots?

The writeups in the old newspapers of the shooting scrapes makes one wonder if they were Bad Men or Bad Shots. The January 1879 paper under Correspondence:

They have some very poor marksmen in Bodie, and some resident undertaker ought to start a shooting gallery there. About 2 o'clock last Monday morning, two men emptied the contents of two six-shooters at each other across the counter of the barroom, with no other effect than tapping a barrel of ale. One of the men then retired to the street, where he obtained a fresh supply of ammunition and, the firing was kept up until nearly daylight, putting three balls through the glass doors and shooting of a cigar in the mouth of a passing stranger, making the cigar too short to smoke. This indignity caused the smoker to lose his temper and he woke up the constable, whereupon the firing ceased.

BODIE EVENING MINER of March 18, 1884

Bodie Camp Coming to the Front. At five o'clock this morning Billy Deegan and Felix Donnelly had a duel on Main Street, at long range. Nine shots were exchanged, but nobody was hurt, not even a bystander was killed—and at that early hour there were many standing around ready to catch any stray ball that came their way. The reason of this great familiarity will be divulged in the examination tomorrow. Both men are at the Hotel de Massey.

There is not a case of sickness in Bodie and were it not for the numerous shooting affrays that keep up a supply of wounded, our physicians could take a rest.

THE BAD MAN FROM BODIE

Oro Mine

The wickedest men, the widest streets and the worst climate—was Bodie's boast. A booming mining town attracts every conceivable type of character and the rough conditions, the lawless atmosphere plus the unrestrained attitude of the times brought out not only the worst, but also the best of the individuals. Bodie soon was associated with descriptions such as: "The Bad Man from Bodie," "The Wickedest Town in the Old West," "Shooters Town," "A Man for Breakfast" (which referred to the day to day murders that occurred in Bodie).

The ARGONAUT of June 1878 first brought out the story of "The Bad Man from Bodie" and it was reprinted in the BODIE WEEKLY STANDARD—thus began a legend. It was the good people, the industrious people, the honest people, the hardworking people who kept the town progressing and yet perhaps this legend of the "Bad Man from Bodie" served a purpose. For it was this notorious reputation that kept Bodie in the eyes of the world and eventually led to Bodie being made a California State Park so Bodie will continue to live not only in legend but also in fact.

Without a doubt there were notorious characters who lived in Bodie and very few County murderers ever heard the death sentence. The editor of the FREE PRESS was quoted as saying, "Their knowledge of it was purely academic."

An incensed editor wrote in January 1880.

Crime Rampant. There is a state of high carnival of crime in Bodie. Within a fortnight two men have been seriously beaten over the head with six shooters, one has been shot to death, one man and one woman have been knifed, one woman's skull crushed with a club, and she may die tonight. For these seven crimes—for these five lives jeopardized and two taken—two arrests have been made. We have constables and several deputies, whose sworn duty it is to enforce the law—and ever so many night watchmen, or private policeman, paid by property owners; and yet crime runs riot nightly in the criminal quarters of the town, and few arrests are made. The patience of the community is commendable. With possibly one exception, everyone of the several hundred instances on the Coast in which the people have been forced to adopt means outside of the law to protect society, the fault has been traceable to the non-performance of duty on the part of the officers of the law.

A glance at the disproportion of our industrial to the idle and dissolute population will convince even the casual observer that we have an unhealthy if not dangerous state of society in Bodie at the present time, and our officers should therefore exercise extra vigilance in the detection and punishment of Crime.

The newspapers of 1880 also report:

Three murders within the last three days, two being the result of the faro bank operators excluding the opium fiends.

Stage robbers have held up one or the other of the various stage lines four times within one week. One of the robbers was killed by a messenger, who in turn, is himself severely wounded.

CARSON CITY NEWS, May 26, 1914

Old Pioneer Writes of Cleaning up Bodie by famous "601"

The day of Judge Lynch has passed but in his day he was the greatest factor for the cleaning up of a community that has ever been known and while there have been a number of instances reported wherein the Judge erred yet as a general rule his mandates were of lasting benefit to the community . . .

A time arose in Bodie these killings were becoming far too frequent and the killers were stepping out of their ranks and were placing the toes of the good men toward the daisies . . .

A cold blooded assasination took place after a New Year's Dance when Joseph DeRoche, persisted in dancing with Mrs. Treloar over the objections of her husband, Tommy Treloar. Mr. Treloar left the dance to go home to build a fire and was followed outside by "Frenchy" DeRoche who deliberately shot him in the back at the corner of Lowe and Main streets. DeRoche was arrested at once, but escaped from the deputy. Citizens formed the "601" and set out in search of the escapee. DeRoche was captured at the goat ranch and returned to Bodie after the group voted by one vote that he should be taken to Bodie instead of Bridgeport. DeRoche was placed in jail and the posse went home to sleep. Shortly after midnight the members of the "601" met at Boone's corrals and marched to the jail which they surrounded. Masked leaders told the sheriff they had come for DeRoche . . . Six men walked into the building and unlocked the cell in which DeRoche was confined. DeRoche arose from his bunk and pulled on his boots. A canvas coat was picked up and thrown over his shoulders and he was marched out. The man never spoke while he was being forced to get up, dress and leave

Original Summit

the building. He was marched out the door and to the center of the "601" who formed a square around him. The body of men marched up Bonanza Street, thence down King Street to Main and from Main to Green where they turned onto Lowe Street and marched to the front of the Fred Weber's blacksmith shop. At a command the men lifted the big wagon jack from its foundation and marched along with it to the spot where the lifeblood of Treloar had stained the ice and snow to a dark red. DeRoche was marched upon the crimson spot, the rope adjusted around his neck by a brawny blacksmith who, when interrupted in his work by another member of the "601" said, "I know what I'm doing, I adjusted five of these in Aurora."

When all was in readiness, the condemned man was asked if he had anything to say. His only reply was "Oh, my God!" The word was given and the men who were ranged out along the line of the fall of rope walked away, and DeRoche was lifted into the air. The body twitched for a few moments and all was still save the swinging back and forward of the body in the night air.

All was silence. Some twenty masked men armed with rifles and shotguns had formed a circle around the principals of the hanging and facing the gathered crowd kept them back until the work was done . . .

The "601" of Bodie continued its work for several years but were not called upon to do any more hanging. An offical communication received by a person of Bodie, bearing the fatal signature of "601", countersigned with the number of the secretary, was a sufficient inducement for that person to change his place of residence and there were many who did not wait for the invitation.

The Law and Order League, did its best to stay the work of the "601" but after the shooting of several members of the organization of the League, after a meeting, their efforts were in vain, and the promiscuous killings were at an end. It is true that scores of men were killed afterwards in the town of Bodie but each was given some semblance of a trial and many were sent to prison. The day of the "bad man" was ended, however, and those who had notches on their guns, kept their guns hidden and forgot the combination to the trigger.

The Bad Boys were Followed by
The Bad Girls

Among the inhabitants of "Virgin Alley" and "Maiden Lane" were the demimondaines Rosa Mae of the Highgrade, Emma Goldsmith of the Ozark, Beautiful Doll and Madame Moustache. The BODIE WEEKLY STANDARD of May 29, 1878:

> Madame Moustache. After visiting nearly every camp in Montana, Idaho and Nevada, Madame Moustache, whose real name is Eleanor Dumont, has settled for the time in Bodie, following her old avocation of dealing in 21, faro, etc. as the forces of circumstances seem to demand. Probably no woman on the Pacific Coast is better known. She has been in a great many of the camps when at their height of prosperity and excitement and remained until there hardly was a dog there to wail out the dismal story of their desertion. She appears as young as ever, and those who knew her ever so many years ago would instantly recognize her now.

A later story in the newspapers tells of the suicide of Eleanor Dumont—thus ended the career of Madame Moustache.

Other inhabitants from the houses of ill repute were newspaper copy, too.

> In addition to two sirens of easy conscience being pitched out of a saloon, head first through a glass door, and a terrific war of words, which with all the expletives known to seven languages were exchanged, on Virtue Street, no other transgressions are reported this morning.

> Rosa Oalaque, the demimonde, slashed John Green across the face, inflicting a deep gash from his right eye to his left chin. Green having only a pen knife stabbed the woman several times in the arm. Both were arrested and when up for examination, the testimony went to show that one was as much to blame as the other so both were discharged.

> The Cyprian on the Rampage. Rosa Oalaque, the same Spanish maid that slashed John Green across the face got full of fighting whiskey, donned her warpaint and started out to clean out (the soiled) dovecotes on Bonanza Street, Thanksgiving night. The officers put her in a little bed in jail, where she remains at present.

BODIE EVENING MINER.

SATURDAY, FEBRUARY 23, 1884.

SLICKENS.

The Sweet Slobberings of a Miner Reporter.

We have had another snow storm and the bleak winds of this morning reminds us more of December than May, but Pat Beggan can warm the inner man for you with drinks fit for the gods.

~~Mike Schwartz~~ will ~~~~

The drivers of Cain & Stewart's wood sleighs have had a tough time of it the last few days breaking trails to peoples' houses, with supplies of wood, but there was no increase in prices on that account.

Didn't Want To Be Killed In Lent.

A wild steer, in Kirman & Rickey's slaughter house corral. concluding that he ought not to be killed during Lent, and being assisted by the corral being nearly full of snow, jumped out yesterday, while E. Johl was killing some of his brethren, and came up town to act as roadbreaker, and to see the boys and dogs; seventeen of the latter met him at the lower end of Main street and escorted him through town several times, assisted by men and boys who lined the sidewalks, and who kept the steer crazed with yells and snowballs; but Mr. Steer frequntly made a lively scattering among his brave foes. Mistaking a Chinaman for a beefeater he charged on him; the Chinaman received him on one of his baskets and the only reason why that Chinaman can washee today is that the deep snow threw the steer down and John escaped. Soon E. Johl came along with his little gun and killed the brute and dressed him in the street, and Eli's knife flew around that beef like a cooper around a barrel and soon the steer was hung where the dogs couldn't reach him.

Full Costumed Bonbon Party.

There was no end of sport at the Miners' Union Hall last Saturday evening at Brofessor Carroll's beanoguessibus soiree. The ladies and gentlemen, from the Odd Fellows' party kept alternating between the two halls so both halls were comfortably filled. Dr Anderson, Charley Taylor, and Mr. Lane were elected Counts (for that evening only). There were 606 beans in the chicita saco, and as Mrs. Sabin had estimated the number at 600 the prize bracelets were attached to her wrists. Mrs. Henderson thought that there ought to be 1200 or 12,000 (we can't say which); for such sound judgment the Counts felt justified in presenting her With The Six Hundred And Six Beans. At the next Saturday evening soiree everybody will receive a present of a full costume, contained in a bonbon.

THE LAUREL PALACE ~~~~

Professor Carroll's practicing class, for gentlemen learning to dance, assembles this afternoon and evening.

Bodie's Second Sunday In Lent.

Saturday we all hoped the snow for this Winter, or Spring rather, was over, but Saturday evening snow commenced falling again and by Sunday noon two feet more of the beautiful had been ad- ded to the unusually large supply already on hand. Then the clerk of the weather gave the boys five hours of sunshine in which to shovel snow off the overburden- ed roofs and porches. At five o'clock the storm commenced again in all its fury, and lasted until half past four o'clock this morning, accompanied by very high winds which would have knocked many a Bodie palace galleywest had they not been weighted down with snow.

An Irish gentleman is reported to have . . . . . the Muni . . .

Mr. Reinstein arrived on the Haw- thorne stage yesterday.

Miss Sarah D. Hector left yesterday on the Hawthorne coach. This young lady has resided a long time in Bodie and has made hosts of friends who deeply regret her departure, but at the same time they desire to tender congratulations and good wishes for her future. We are informed that Miss H. will travel North, from San Francisco, as Mrs. M.

Friday evening George Courtnage was installed as Vice Chancellor of the Knights of Pythias. If George is pos- sessed of vice enough to make a good Vice Chancellor what a pre-eminent C. C. he would make.

Wm. A. Irwin and J. Wells went down on yesterday's Hawthorne stage.

Harry Reinstein is M. P. Wolf's new clerk.

A. Huntoon and family have returned home.

EIGHTEENTH ANNIVERSARY
Masquerade Ball
⊱ TO BE GIVEN BY ⊰
COUNCIL of the P. P. P. No. 33,333,
⊰ AT ⊱
MINERS' UNION HALL,
⊰ ON ⊱
MONDAY EVENING, FEBRUARY 22, 1897.
⊐ TICKETS, TWO DOLLARS. ⊏

CENTRAL SALOON.
Andrew Carion
Will open the
Central Saloon as a Depot for Bodie Brewery Beer,
And will keep in addition all kinds of Liquors and Cigars of excellent quality. (Formerly the Chicago Brewery Saloon.)   ap3   A. A. CARION, Proprietor.

PAROLE SALOON.
MORT CULLINAN, Proprietor.
This old and popular resort furnishes as fine Wines Liquors, Cigars, and Beers as can be had in the mountains. Club and reading rooms attached.   d21

Fine Furnished Rooms

NO MORE COLD WATER.—Joe Vieira has now got his elegant baths worked square up to the top cock of hot water. Joe, in his new house, is giving elegant baths and nice shaving, hair cutting, and shampooing.

Across the street from Van Voorhies is a finely developed snowbank. Behind this Arctic outfit the careful searcher will find Fred Henseleit's tailor shop; he can make you a fashionable suit in the latest styles of goods or he will repair your old clothes, making them look almost as good as new.

P P P.—L. Cohn has just received a large assortment of masks for the masquerade ball on the 22d. Those who call early will get the first choice.

This cold, stormy, disagreeable weath-

---

character first rate.

Mrs. James Henderson—"May Queen" —Dressed very attractively.

Miss Adah Harrington—"Gipsey"— Took the romance out of the tribe by appearing as a very fascinating one.

Eli Johl—Appeared as Eli Johl in a black domino.

Mrs. Eli Johl—"Flower Girl"—This lady's costume was very much admired.

Mrs. Lucy Johns—"Cure for love"— Presented a marvellously attractive appearance in a costume ornamented with numerous mittens. Original and elegant.

H Kelly—First, aid full justice the character.

R. J. Williamson—Made a fine looking "Vaquero."

Miss Helen Watson—Looked every inch a "Gipsey Queen."

Mrs. J. H. Warren—Domino.

Miss Lizzie Watson—Domino.

Dr. D. Walker—"P P P P"—That is, the Doctor went them one P. better.

Miss C. Walker—"Painting."

[But for the unfortunate loss of their notebooks by nine of our reporters this report would be more elaborate.—EDITOR MINER.]

Leaving Out the Joke.

It was a burning shame to slaughter those twenty pet steers, but "Sel" Warren said, "pets or no pets my customers must and shall have the best the country affords". It will gratify the lovers of fine beef to call into the City Market and inspect what the hooks are loaded with.

FIRE

September 21, 1878

Our precautions against fire, we are pleased to see, has been acted on in several instances. But much more remains to be done in that direction. By procuring empty barrels or tin cans, filling them with water and placing them around or on top of houses, a serious conflagration can be checked in its incipiency. We trust our property-holders will see the necessity of immediate and prompt action in this matter, as each and every one of them are more or less interested in the safety of our town from fire.

December 1879
THE WATER WORKS

Should the weather prove favorable, the pipe will all be laid from the large reservoir on the hill to Main Street within a few days. Gill-

Postcards by Frasher of the June 23, 1932 Bodie fire.
Courtesy of William Glenn

son & Barber are manufacturing the pipe in their shop in Bodie, having a corps of twelve pipe makers employed on the job.

The water will be supplied from the Mono mine through a 10" pipe, 300 feet distant from the reservoir. A 10 inch pipe leads from the reservoir down the hill for a distance of 500 feet, then the size of the pipe diminishes to 6 inches for a distance of 2000 feet. The hose carts are being manufactured in San Francisco. When this improvement is completed our fears of a holocaust will vanish.

THE FIRE BOYS

Now that the water mains are about completed and Bodie has at last adequate fire protection, there is great interest manifest in organizing hose companies. The Neptune Hose Company, No. 1, with 56 names, was launched with great enthusiasm, as was Champion Hose Company, No. 1.

SHUT HIMSELF OUT

When the fire bell sounded the alarm at 2 o'clock Monday morning, a barber doing business not a thousand miles from McGee's Exchange, rushed out into the street, clad in his night shirt only, closing the night latched door behind him and leaving the key inside. As soon as the frosty atmosphere enveloped him he turned to seek his warm bed, but could not enter. A German shoemaker slept in the back room, and, after hammering at the front door until he was nearly frozen, the barber procured a pick handle, ascending to the roof, shinned along it until he came to a spot immediately above the sleeping Crespian, and there he sat beating upon the roof with his pick handle

until the whole neighborhood was aroused, but the shoemaker continued to snore like a steam saw mill. His feet and fingers, being nearly frozen and his whole frame chilled thoroughly, the barber grew desperate, and descending to the sidewalk he procured a pick and burst in his door. He has sworn off running to fires in his night shirt.

INYO REGISTER, Thursday,, July 28, 1892

The BODIE MINER was completely burned out, but Bro. Morgan was enabled to Phoenix out his regular issue on time through the kindness of the Chronicle-Union. The MINER has ordered a new outfit.

BODIE'S GREAT FIRE

CHRONICLE-UNION, Bridgeport, July 30, 1892

We gather the following account of the fire in Bodie from yesterday's BODIE MINER:

The fire started in the building used by Mrs. James Perry as a grocery store, restaurant and bakery. It was about 2 o'clock in the morning when the Chinese cook discovered the blaze, and at once an alarm was given. Assistance was soon at hand, but the flames were spreading so quickly, it was found impossible to check them with the water on the premises, and attention was given to saving of the contents of the house. The heat was so oppressive, however, little in this direction was accomplished.

The buildings on either side of Mrs. Perry's soon caught, and from one place to another the flames leaped, it becoming more apparent every minute that the greater part of the west side of the street was doomed.

It was but a short time before the Goodson buildings and Occidental Hotel, on the e a s t side of the street, were ablaze, then it was all hope departed.

In the meantime, as soon as the alarm was given, the fireman got out the hose carts and hook and ladder truck, and attached hose to the hydrants. But there was no water.

While waiting for the water from the reservoir the men busied themselves getting what they could from wells, pumps and the like in an attempt to keep the fire from buildings that were not yet burning. But their efforts were vain. On rushed the relentless flames, seemingly taking a fiendish delight in destroying as much property as possible.

Water! Water! The only salvation of the town, where is it? Why was none on the scene?

Quickly spread the rumor that there was none in the reservoir, but this proved to be untrue. The reservoir was full, but someone had blundered. Each second this blunder was becoming more costly to the people.

Finally the rushing sound of the water was heard, bringing with it a ray of hope to those whose property thus far had escaped. But alas! It was too late to save the business portion of the town. Nearly the entire length of Main Street was a sheet of blazing fire.

Bravely and manfully the firemen went to work perserveringly laboring to keep the flames from spreading further. They worked with might and main, and to their noble efforts many a family is indebted for sheltering homes today. Many times it was feared that despite their efforts, different residents would follow the business houses and be burned to the ground, but this thought proved erroneous.

The defiant flames, so unconquerable for a while, were at last subdued and gotton under control.

Day dawned upon a scene of desolation. Where once had stood

prosperous business houses now nothing remained but their ruins. Main Street presented a sorry sight. For nearly its entire length nothing met the eye but the debris of burned buildings. Scattered about in different places at a safe distance from the street were the things that had been saved. They comprised a miscellaneous assortment and included a little of everything, from a piano to a paper of pins.

Not an eating house nor a lodging house was left, and numerous miners and others were left without places to sleep or procure breakfast; but the private families overcame this difficulty by placing their homes at the disposal of the unfortunates, so none went without food or shelter.

Early in the morning a grand scramble took place for buildings, and places that had before been considered worth but little became valuable. Everything in the shape of a house is being utilized for some purpose. A number of unoccupied buildings were standing in different parts of town and these will be moved to the old lots, or new ones will be built. Some of the businessmen are yet undecided as to where they will locate, but most of them will probably start at their old places.

The cause of fire is shrouded in mystery, but there are some circumstances that point to the hand of the incendiary. As stated above, the first one to see the blaze was a Chinese cook employed by Mrs. Perry. As soon as he entered the kitchen he smelled the fumes of coal oil, and at the same time noticed flames leaping up from a large meat block, which is similar to those used in butcher shops. The second person in the room was P. Walheim, who also states that there was a strong odor of coal oil. At first it was thought that the fire had started in the bakery part of the building, but this was not the case. It was in the kitchen, and as there was no fire in the range or bakery, nor had there been since the previous evening, it looks suspicious, to say the least.

You will remember that about the same time in the morning on July 5th a fire broke out in nearly the same place as this last one. The first one was easily extinguished by few buckets of water. At the time it was not exactly clear how the fire started but in view of the light of subsequent events it is easy to believe it was incendiary in its origin. It requires no great excursion of the mind to connect the two fires, and to imagine that they were the work of some person who is bent upon a spirit of revenge against Mrs. Perry or her family. It is hard to contemplate a being so devoid of all principles of manhood and humanity as to willfully and deliberately endanger lives and property of hundreds of people; but it is a painful fact that such have existed and do exist at this time.

The property saved from the burned houses amounted to but little. Some goods were taken out of the places on the west side of the street, but much thus saved was afterward burned or stolen. On the other side, the people had placed all hopes in the timely arrival of the water, but little effort was made to have things taken to a place of safety until it was too late to accomplish much.

Through the stupidity or ignorance of someone the water was not there in time. The town gets its water for fire purposes from a reservoir on the hill, which is supplied by the Lent Shaft. At the Standard Mill is a water gate to let the water into the pipes into town, so all that is necessary in case of fire is to turn it out there; but the arrangement is such that one unfamiliar with its working would turn the water off instead of on. On this occasion the water was probably turned on by Joseph Beck, the Standard Mill watchman, who went about his regular duties. Someone from town then arrived and, thinking that the water had not been turned on, proceeded to do so as he thought, but really turned it off. In this way very valuable time was lost.

List of losses . . . The above figures, although aggregating $88,-100.00 do not represent the entire loss . . . etc.

In all there were 64 buildings destroyed, and the burned district extends from the shed south where Andrew Arrild's Livery Stable was to Cain's bank on the west side of Main Street; and on the east side from A. Soldering's Assay Office to the old dwelling house of Silas B. Smith, but which is now owned by John Langrell.

CU April 29, 1893

A Fire Company—As the fire apparatus has been shipped from San Francisco and a company to take charge of it—They should have weekly drills so as to be proficient in handling the ladders, etc., so in case we should be so unfortunate to have a fire they would know how to work efficiently. If the apparatus is what it is represented to be, it can be handily run to any part of the town and be the means of saving much property in case of fire. Get a move on, Boys, and organize your company.

BRIDGEPORT CHRONICLE-UNION and BODIE CHRONICLE, Bridgeport, June 25, 1932

DISASTROUS FIRE AT BODIE

Entire Main Street Swept by Flames; Little Remains of Historic Town's Business Section.

FAMOUS OLD MINING CAMP IN RUNS FOR THE THIRD TIME BY FIRE

The famous old mining camp of Bodie was visited by the third great fire of its history on Thursday afternoon June 23.

The fire, which was said to have started in a house in the rear of the Old Sawdust Corner Saloon, spread rapidly from building to building and first from one side of Main Street to the other, until from the Hydro Building on the east side of Main Street down street toward the north the fire spread, destroying such old familiar buildings on that side of the street, such as the U.S. Hotel, the Occidental Hotel, and to the Masonic Hall, together with the Joe Seri home and other buildings.

On the opposite side of the street the famous old bank building owned by J. S. Cain which had successfully withstood the ravages of the other two great fires visiting the old camp, the post office building adjoining it, the Old Sawdust Corner Saloon, owned by the Langrell Brothers, and Bodie Club, Butterfly Resort, and several other buildings on the west side of Main Street and the next street west, all went down in Thursday's great fire.

At the time the alarm sounded, most of the men were in the mines at work and did not know until they were warned of the great danger that threatened the old town. George Moyle and a few of the boys around town got out the first hose lines, and it is said also, that a couple of the ladies of the town also got out on the hose carts in their eagerness to help quell the Demon Fire, but with rocks coming through the hydrants and clogging pipes and fire hose nozzles, the fight was a losing one from the start.

Sam Leon, owner of the U. S. Hotel, took his truck to help move someone's belongings from the fire zone thinking his own property safe and had moved his loaded truck to a safety zone, when his attention was called to the fact that the fire had settled down on his Hotel building and all he saved, we were informed, was his truck, the entire building and its contents going up in smoke.

Hard and close work saved the homes of several in the fire zone and most of the folks hurriedly moved their treasured possessions beyond the fire's reach.

When word came over the telephone to Bridgeport, advising of the old mining town's sad plight, a number of our citizens, rushed to the rescue, to try to do everything possible to save some of the buildings but by the time they covered the 20 miles to the town of Bodie, the damage had been done, and all they then could do was to help put out the smoldering ruins in an effort to keep the fire from spreading to untouched property, and when it was considered safe to do so, the hose line was run down the street to the old bank building and water poured upon the bank vault in hopes that its valuable records and other contents would be saved. As it would be several days before the vault is cooled sufficiently for it to be opened it will not be known whether its construction was of such a character as to safeguard its contents. In the shells of several of the buildings left in the fire a number of safes were noted, but it was not known whether they held valuables or not.

The cause of the fire is said to have been due to the fact a little boy was playing with matches in the absence of his parents.

At the time the fire started, most of the ladies 'round town were at the local school house at which a party was given by the teacher, Mrs. D. Victor Cain.

From the standpoint of loss, those of J. S. Cain exceed the loss of all the property owners and while some insurance was carried on some of the buildings that went down in Thursday evening's holocaust, it is not known at the time of our going to press, just to what extent the losses are covered by insurance.

Someone has written on the stone

"BODIE AFIRE" JUNE 23, 1932
BODIE, MONO COUNTY, CALIF.

which has in the past been used for drilling contests on M a i n Street, "Bodie died in 1931," but believe it, or not, stranger, as long as "thars gold in them thar hills" which circle the old camp she is not dead, and may yet rise from her ashes as a great producing gold camp. Time will tell. Here's hoping and wishing for the best!

A mining expert—a man who can talk about formations, ramifications, stratifications, tag stones, dips, spurs, angles, tilt lines, outside sediments, and all other ites and tites.

A tenderfoot—a wooly-boy, just out from the east. Carries his small arms with him, goes prospecting with a shotgun and fishing rod. Buys a salted mine and borrows money from Mother to go home in the fall.

An amalgamater—a man who wears his fingernails long, draws five dollars a shift and deposits $10 in a bank every day. He uses the ore's low grade in warranty and proportion.

A prospector—a man who has a hole in the ground, and the biggest liar in town.

Proposition man—one who wears laced boots and corduroy clothes and never pays his board bill.

All miners are not successful, but many dig in vein.

If seven days makes one week, how many weeks does it take to make one strong?

Some men imagine that they can't sow their wild oats without moistening them with old rye. Black eyes denote passion. It is generally safe to say that the man with a black eye has angered someone.

If a Bodie meet a Bodie
And a Bodie's dry,
If a Bodie treat a Bodie
Let him treat to rye.

South Bodie Mine

The Standard

1861 —Bunker Hill Mine owned by L. H. Dearborn, O. G. Leach and E. Donahue.

—Later was sold to James Stark and John W. Tucker who called it "Opera House Mill" as Stark owned a theatre in San Jose and wanted to convert it into a mill to be used at this Bodie mine.

—Then was sold to Aurora Company.

1863 —Bodie Bluff Consolidated Mining Company organized and for $1,100,000 by Judge F. T. Bechtel and Leland Stanford.

—Mining grounds came into the hands of four men: Essington, Lockwood, Mooney and Walker.

—Mooney and Walker quit the unpaying partnership.

1865 —William O'Hara, a colored man, kept a boarding house and also was a night watchman at a mine.

—Boarders Essington and Lockwood owned Bunker Hill claim and operated a small arrastra on Rough Creek. Owed board and borrowed money from O'Hara in the amount of $950 so gave O'Hara deed to the mine.

—O'Hara unable to sell the mine at any price.

1874 —Peter Essington and Lewis Lockwood returned. O'Hara gave them back the deed and they again worked the mine and the arrastra. The partners were to pay $8000 to O'Hara out of mine earnings.

—Either because they lacked money to buy proper shoring or through pure luck, the partners arrived at the mine one morning to see that there had been a cave in . . . and this cave in exposed a rich chamber of ore which made the Standard famous. The men re-located to form the Bullion and Bunker claims. Partners took out $37,000 and then sold to:

Copied from old photograph captioned "The Standard Mill."

Original Standard Mill
Courtesy of McDonell sisters

Cyanide Plant at the Standard Mine.
A. A. Forbes Photo
Courtesy of Los Angeles County Museum

1876 —Cook brothers, Dan and Seth, Col. John F. Boyd and William Lent for $65,000. The STANDARD MINING COMPANY was formed in April 1877. During its first year of operation, this company paid off purchase price of $65,000 plus all equipment purchased and mining expenses. This began to awaken the mining world to Bodie's possibilities. Ore was treated at the Syndicate Mill. Standard later erected its own 20-stamp mill (using parts of the Del Monte Mill of Aurora). A 2500 foot tramway was built to the mill. During the first 7 years the Standard Mine yielded eleven million dollars and the company paid three and one-half million in dividends.

1878 —Bodie Mining Company adjoined the Standard; from there came word of a rich gold and silver strike that startled the world. Ore was so rich that guards rode with the ore wagons and guards stayed at the mill.

1887 —Standard and Bodie mines merged.

1899 —Standard Mill burned down
—New 20-stamp mill built to replace the loss

1909 —Standard Consolidated was opened to leasers.

1915 —Standard Mining property taken over by J. S. Cain Company.

1929 —Treadwell Yukon took a lease on every property in camp.

1935 —Spreckel's Sugar Company leased mining interests on Standard Hill from J. S. Cain Company until war closed down operation. New mill was built at this time.

1947 —Work was resumed until fire demolished the mill

Crew out in front of the Standard.
Courtesy of McDonell sisters

The ruins of the Standard Mill after the fire.
Harry Metzger and McDonell sisters

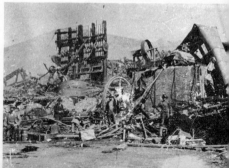

Gold bullion

BULLION SHIPMENTS

1877

Standard	$ 784,522.60
Mexican	
Red Cloud	12,500.00
Kate Rogers	

1878

Standard Con.,	1,025,383.35
Bodie Con.,	1,042,236.80
Bechtel	58,634.93
Red Cloud	1,927.50
Scattering	1,550.00
	2,129,732.58

1879

Standard Con.,	1,448,845.47
Bodie Con.	784,077.12
Bulwer Con.	241,094.38
Noonday	36,532.29
Syndicate	12,318.38
Bechtel Con.	11,506.85
Sitting Bull	3,485.00
By Banks	39,000.00
	2,556,847.58

1880

Standard Con.	$1,858,763.46
Noonday	511,757.20
Bodie Con.	529,817.80
Bulwer Con.	117,498.33
Belvidere	25,901.26
Syndicate	24,769.75
Dudley	1,746.06
Scattering	93,445.26
	3,063,699.13

Total for all mines

Standard	5,117,515.08
Bodie	2,236,121.72
Noonday	548,289.50
Bulwer	358,592.71
Bechtel	71,690.98
Syndicate	37,085.93
Belvidere	25,901.26
Red Cloud	10,927.50
Sitting Bull	3,485.09
Mexican	2,000.00
Dudley	1,746.06
Kate Rogers	1,500.00
Scattering	132,445.26
	8,547,301.09

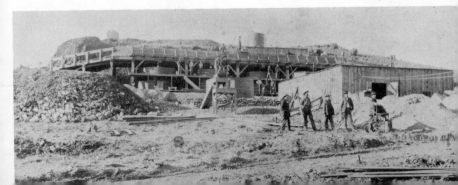

Standard Cyanide Plant from an old sepia print.

County Seat

Ambulatory county seat of Mono

During the heighth of its heyday Aurora was assumed to be in Mono County, California and became the county seat in March 24, 1861; but Aurora was also claimed by the territory of Nevada as the county seat of Esmeralda County. So for a time a surprisingly harmonious dual government existed. The substantial courthouse that was built eventually became the newspaper office.

The boundary survey was unfinished at the time of the September 1863 elections so the Aurora populace gaily voted twice—at Armory Hall for the Esmeralda County officials and at the Police Station on the Mono County Ballot. Later in the month the survey showed Aurora to be in Nevada and Bodie to be in California so some of the County officials loaded the records into wagons and transported them to the still small hamlet of Bodie. In the spring of 1864 a special election was held to determine the county seat at which time Bridgeport was chosen. The records were moved to Bridgeport to Kingsley's Inn which some consider to be the first house to be built in Bridgeport.

Not only is the foundation of the present courthouse built of Bodie granite, but also it is built principally of Bodie money as a 6% property tax had been levied. This Victorian type courthouse was completed in 1881 and is today one of the most charming county seats in California with the interesting addition of a cannon on the lawn which was presented to the County by J. S. Cain. The cannon had been cast in the Standard Machine Shop in Bodie.

Bodie Foundry

Map labels:

TO RENO, NEV.
TO SONORA
TO AURORA, NEV.
NEV. CAL.
BODIE
TO HAWTHORNE, NEV.
Bridgeport
Conway Summit
SIERRA
395
Mono Lake
Lee Vining
TO YOSEMITE
120
NEVADA
Mono Lake
Mono Mills
TO TONOPAH, NEV.
Benton Sta.
Benton
WHITE MTNS.
Mono Craters
6
Owens
Mammoth
Crowley Lake
MONO CO.
INYO CO.
395
Laws
BISHOP
TO LOS ANGELES
MTNS.

Approaching Bodie on the Aurora road, you passed the milk ranch on your right.

A. A. Forbes Photo   Courtesy of Los Angeles County Museum

FORBES   Bodie, Cal 1139

EVELYN,
BELOVED
DAUGHTER OF
FANNIE O.
& ALBERT K.
MYERS,
BORN MAY 1, 1894,
DIED APRIL 5, 1897.

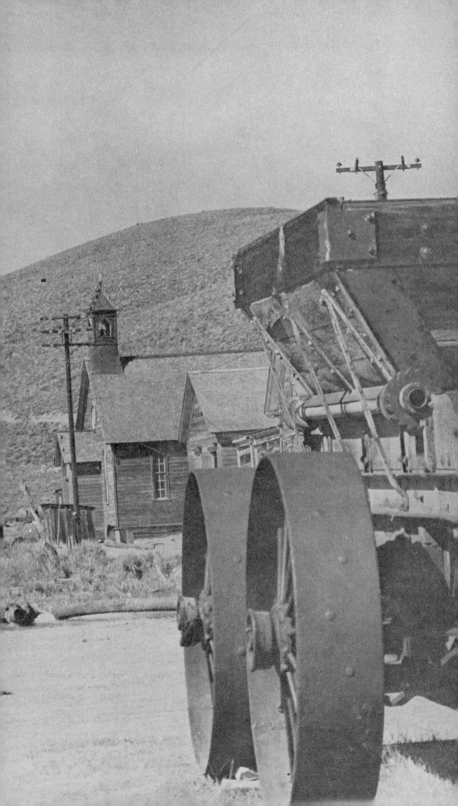

495

Bodie as it appears today.